Bugling for Elk

A Complete Guide to Early-Season Elk Hunting

By Dwight Schuh

Published in the United States of America 1983

Bugling for Elk

A Complete Guide to Early-Season Elk Hunting

Copyright 1983 by Dwight Schuh

Library of Congress Catalog No 83-60907

I.S.B.N. 0-912299-03-7

Dedication

To Larry

THANKS

My sincere thanks goes out to all of those who've helped me learn about elk hunting. Biologists in every western state have generously offered their time and knowledge, and many hunters have shared their tips and secrets. Rather than listing them all here, I have, throughout the book, given credit where credit is due. One person not mentioned deserves special thanks, and that's my wife Laura who, for better and worse, has supported me faithfully.

Table of Contents

Cover Photo: Photographer Joseph V. Kaliszewski of Sisters, Oregon, caught this magnificent bugling bull elk on Kodachrome 64 film in the first five minutes, of sunrise on a foggy September morning. The unusual light occurred as a bright beam of sunlight lit up the area just as a heavy fog opened up.

(Photo courtesy Larry D. Jones)

Bugling for Elk

Introduction

Elk hunting. Does any serious big game hunter not dream of hunting elk? Deer are more numerous than elk, moose are bigger, sheep are more glamorous, bears are more mysterious, yet something about elk turns hunters on and captures their dreams and imaginations. Maybe it's that they're big, brawny, brawling animals that wake a sense of wildness in hunters; that they live in pristine country, America's last frontiers; that they grow huge trophy racks; that they yield mountains of meat. Or that they bugle.

Perhaps it's this last quality above all others that really energizes hunters. Early each fall during the rut, the breeding season, bull elk take on new character. They shed their sleek, brown, well-kept summer appearance, the air of the well-kept businessman, to take on the tousled, pugnacious, brutal, swaggering, uncouth demeanor of ruffians. They roar, bellow and bugle through the woods, tearing up trees and pushing each other around, their necks swollen to the size of oil drums, their eyes bloodshot and fierce, their bodies rank with crusted mud and urine. Maybe this transformation from dignity to depravity triggers a similar metamorphosis in hunters that stirs primordial instincts and draws them unrelentingly to the field. Whatever the cause, you'll find few other big game hunters as feverish and incorrigible as the serious elk bugler. Don't ask where he'll be come September. That dude will be out there bugling for elk.

ABOUT THIS BOOK

The term "early season" refers to the rutting period, which extends roughly from late August through early October. That's the bugling season. By mid-October in most regions, elk quit bugling and withdraw to secret haunts to put on fat for winter. They're different animals then and late seasons of October, November and December bring cold and snow to create different hunting conditions. Late-season hunting is a subject unto itself.

To a great extent early-season hunting means bowhunting because most states allow archery hunting only during the rut. However, some states and provinces do hold rifle seasons for bugling bulls, especially in backcountry units, and some have special muzzleloader seasons. So while my comments reveal a strong bowhunting slant, they're apropos to all hunting for bugling elk.

This book is written strictly for hunters. It's complete in the sense that it covers all aspects of early-season hunting, but it doesn't encompass the life history of elk or explain why elk are really wapiti or whatever. That all may be interesting, but it has no bearing on duking it out with a lusty bull on a lonely mountain. My emphasis rests solely on bugling a bull within rifle or bow range and other subjects related to hunting the unique early-fall period.

ELK HUNTING TODAY

Bugling for Elk was born of the times. At this writing no other book on the market deals solely with bugling for elk, yet this may be today's hottest hunting subject. Elk herds have never been in better shape than right now. Every western state has growing herds, and most states continue to build elk numbers through special regulations and transplanting of animals to new areas. In many cases logging has opened up old-growth forests to the benefit of elk, and range management that stresses grass production generally has helped elk. In Colorado and other states elk have spread on their own to establish new populations in regions traditionally considered as marginal habitat. As big powerful animals, elk aren't subject to fluctuations caused by winter kill and predation as deer are. In short, we're living right now in the good ol' days of elk hunting.

Along with that, seasons have been liberalized. States such as Wyoming, Montana and Idaho traditionally have held backcountry rifle hunts during the rut, but these are beyond the financial or physical means of many hunters. With the exploding popularity of archery tackle and muzzleloaders for hunting, most elk states have adopted primitive-weapons seasons during the rut in virtually all country that holds elk, and this trend has put the opportunity to bugle for elk within the reach of all hunters.

A PERSONAL GLIMPSE

It was this seeming glorious opportunity that first drew me to elk hunting in the early 1970s. I'd launched my career as an outdoor writer, and hunting for elk seemed to only sensible thing to do. Heaven knows, most hunters crave to read the rousing recount of a skirmish between man and beast, so what other choice was there? I told all who would listen that I was going out to bugle up a bull. Whew! That was heady stuff. Big time.

I drove 400 miles across my home state of Oregon to a spot recommended by a friend in the Blue Mountains, and there I went elk hunting. And hunting. And hunting. Mercifully I'd allowed only the last five days of the season; dragging it out longer than that would have bordered on cruelty. In those five days filled with hiking, searching, bugling and praying, I saw three elk—two cows and a little 3-point bull late the last evening. That was it. I'd heard no bugling.

Needless to say, elk bugling had been disheartening and frustrating. But it wouldn't be forgotten. Despite it's austerity, or perhaps because of it, that hunt had changed me, stirred some subtle innate drive that had never been stirred before. Maybe it was the chance sighting of that bull the last night, the challenge of learning, the anger at being defeated, or a glimpse of snowcapped high country in the distance, but some quality had captured my interest. The seed had been planted, and it was only a matter of time until bugling for elk blossomed as an obsession within.

That could be taken as a warning. Once you try elk hunting you won't be the same. You may swear never to go again, or you may be hooked for life, but one thing is for sure. You won't forget. That's the way it is, this bugling for elk!

Good hunting,

DWIGHT SCHUH
April 1983

To Plan a Hunt

Planning. That's where good elk hunting starts. Stalking and bugling may be the exciting aspects of hunting, but they aren't the core. Over the years, hunting friends and I have had great bugling experiences, but that hasn't necessarily been because we're great buglers. Mostly it's because we've hunted great locations. We've gone to regions with lots of elk and huntable conditions, and we've found those places through planning.

The approach outlined here assumes you'll be hunting new country, so I'll detail the entire planning process. If you live in elk country and know your area, you might take much of this for granted, but that doesn't mean ideas on planning concern beginners only. Some locals assume that nonresidents are blundering fools and that residents know the ropes, but harvest statistics don't bear that out. In all states nonresidents have a higher success rate than residents. That could be true for several reasons, but it does point out one fact—locals don't necessarily have all the answers. While bowhunting in Colorado, two friends and I killed two bulls. As we pulled into restaurants and gas stations, the antlers in our rig attracted much attention. We were more amazed at the amazement of the locals than they were at our success. Living more than 1,000 miles away, we knew more about hunting

If you have no time for planning your own hunt and you have extra money, an outfitted hunt may be ideal for you. The outfitter takes care of all the details, and all you have to do is hunt.

conditions there than most of the people who lived right in the middle of fabulous elk territory.

Often when something exists close by, we become myopic and lose our vision, hunting traditional canyons and mountains year after year, never asking why we might be wise to try somewhere else. Regardless of where you live, look beyond the obvious and assess conditions afresh each year. By making slight adjustments, you might double your pleasure, thrills and success.

THE OUTFITTED HUNT

If your lifestyle leaves little time to do your own planning and you have plenty of money, an outfitted hunt may be ideal for you. You face no concerns but to get to the hunting area and to make a good shot once you get into game.

Assuring a satisfactory hunt with an outfitter is more a matter of precaution than planning. The outfitter will tell you what to bring and what to expect in the way of hunting conditions. It'll go smoothly if you have a reputable outfitter, but that's where precautions come in. Shifty characters have infiltrated every business these days and outfitting, despite its robust, wholesome, outdoorsy mystique, hasn't been immune. Some states have licensing systems that require all guides and outfitters to meet minimum standards, which help to weed out most of the sour apples, but Washington, Oregon, Utah, Colorado and New Mexico have no license system at all, so literally anybody can open up a guiding service there, regardless of qualifications or intent. In most states, outfitters and guides have done an excellent job of policing themselves through their own associations, and certainly many independent outfitters are reputable. But to assure yourself of a first-class hunt, take these precautions: Insist on a contract outlining the terms of the hunt; make sure you understand how many days you'll actually spend hunting and what services the outfitter will perform. Ask for a half-dozen references, including some who didn't kill any game; most any hunter who's killed a 6-point bull will give a glowing report, but the hunter who got skunked will give an honest report. Ask if your outfitter is insured; otherwise, if you're injured during a hunt you're entirely on your own. With this type of investigation, you should enjoy a satisfying hunt.

You can also get such a report from most hunting consultants, whose ability to stay in business is built on arranging a hunter a good hunt with reputable outfitter-guides. A hunting consultant has to serve the interests of his clients to survive. Jack Atcheson, an international hunting consultant based in Butte, Montana, renowned for his elk-hunting ability, suggests that the selection of a good guide can make the difference between going home empty-handed or having the best trophy room in the city.

"A consultant wants you to get game," Atcheson said, "so you'll book with him again next year... And the best known reason for hunters to take an outfitted hunt is that guided hunters see and get more game."

HUNTING ON YOUR OWN

Way back when someone started the myth that the outfitted wilderness hunt is the Cadillac of all hunting trips, the ultimate, the hunt of a lifetime, the dream hunt. That myth has been perpetuated until many hunters take it as law. As I've said, the outfitted hunt is tailor-made for some individuals, but it's not perfect for everybody. In fact, I think if you have time to do your own planning, have the initiative to figure things out for yourself, and like to do your own work in camp and in the field, then you can have a better hunt on your own.

Time is one reason. Most guided hunts restrict your hunting time to six to ten days, which limits your flexibility. Because of the demanding, time-consuming nature of elk hunting, I think a trip for these animals should be ten days to two weeks long. At least I think that's true for bowhunters who require, on the average, more time to bag an animal than rifle hunters do.

Also, on some guided hunts you're stuck with hunting only one area, and you're stuck with hunting one way—the guide's way. That's great if he's a student of hunting, but some guides are basically cowboys who moonlight as guides. In my opinion, if you really study elk hunting and learn the fine points of bugling for yourself, you can hunt more effectively on your own than you can with many guides.

PLANNING A HUNT

Books and magazines, harvest statistics, maps, and people underlie planning. To start, set up file folders for each state you're interested in. Then read magazine articles and books, and photocopy any item that gives even a slight clue about hunting in a particular region. File these items in the appropriate folders.

Write to every elk state for hunting regulations. Seasons vary greatly, so without all the regulations you can't even pick the best state. You may find that Colorado, despite its reputation, isn't the best place for you to hunt. Addresses for game departments are listed in Appendix 1.

In writing to game departments, also ask for harvest statistics. Colorado offers a comprehensive book called "Colorado Big Game Harvest," which reads like a Bible of big game hunting in Colorado. To my knowledge no other state publishes anything equal, but all states keep hunting statistics and data from biological surveys, and it's all public

For planning your own hunt, maps are essential. To create a clear mental picture of your intended hunting country, you must have two kinds of maps: Public-land maps, such as these put out by the U.S. Forest Service, and topographic maps, such as the map of Idaho shown here.

information, so inquire about its availability. These data aren't magic, but they'll give you a broad idea of game and hunter distribution, which is a good starting point for further planning.

MAPS

The idea behind planning is to acquire a picture of your hunting territory. If you live close, you can drive out to look it over, but if you live far away you have to create a mental picture, and to do that you need two kinds of maps: public-land maps and topographic maps.

For elk hunting, two public agencies are most significant: the U.S. Forest Service and Bureau of Land Management. Some states also own large blocks of good elk land. These agencies publish maps of their lands, and these are invaluable for showing man-made structures and features—roads, trails, campgrounds, ownership boundaries, national parks, wilderness areas and so forth. You also can get a general idea of natural features from them. Public-land maps generally are more up-to-date than topographic maps, but remember that with today's rapid development, every map is outdated even before it's published. I'll say more about that later.

The idea of using topographic maps in hunting is no big secret. Half the articles ever written about hunting emphasize the value of maps, but many of them stop short. They suggest buying only detailed quadrangle maps for use while hunting, which is excellent advice. But for broad range planning, the area covered by quadrangle maps is too small; you'd have to buy dozens of them for initial planning, so I'd suggest you hold off ordering quadrangle maps until you know precisely where you'll hunt. Then get them!

To discover the array of topographic maps available, write to the U.S. Geological Survey for free order maps of each state. These give all the details of ordering further maps. Two of the most valuable are state and regional topographic maps.

State maps don't show much detail, of course, but they offer a broad view of a state—mountain ranges and valleys, canyons and plateaus—and some of my finest hunts have been inspired simply by my scanning state maps to learn the nature of the country. Regional maps have a scale of 1:250,000. They show more detail than state maps but still cover a wide enough area for planning. By poring over these maps and comparing them with ideas you've acquired from reading and from harvest statistics, you'll begin to formulate concepts, to develop a picture of potential hunting regions.

TALKING TO PEOPLE

That's the beginning. Everything up until now prepares you for the final stage of planning—talking to people. So far you can only assume what a piece of country is like. By talking to someone who's been there, you can fill in the blanks to complete your mental picture. Talking to a person who's intimately familiar with a region is the next best thing to being there yourself.

However, there are good reasons for doing "paper" research first. For one thing, most people will eagerly help someone who's paid his dues, but if they think you're just looking for a free lunch they'll clam up faster than a downwind bull. So learn some facts and demonstrate that you've put out some effort.

Just as important, you must ask specific questions. As a journalist I've learned that the answers you get are only as good as the questions you ask. If you ask something general like, "Where's a good place to hunt?" you'll get a response just as general: "Oh, this is all pretty good country." But if you're equipped to ask: "What's the condition of Road 4832? How many elk would you see in a day on Black Ridge? My map shows openings on Highrise Mountain—are those meadows or rockslides?" you'll get specific, useful answers.

Here's a precaution: Never take one person's word for anything. Some people will lie, and others simply don't know what they're talking about. As my friend Mike Cupell said, develop a good "crap detector." The best insurance is to contact diverse sources. If one area starts sounding good, call three or four people about it. If their stories conflict, be suspicious, but if they substantiate each other, you know you're getting hot.

SOURCES

Big game biologists often are the best information sources. If you know which region you want to hunt start at that level, but if you don't, begin by talking to big game biologists at the state office, then work down—pursuing those areas that sound best, through regional, district and area offices. Most state wildlife agencies are organized that way. At each level ask for names of other possible sources, not just biologists. Talk to game wardens, foresters, hunters, farmers—anybody who can give you insight into local conditions.

During any call keep a list of questions handy so you don't leave out anything important, and keep maps at hand for quick reference. Your questions will depend on what you're looking for in a hunt and on what you've learned through initial research, but some general topics apply to all planning.

BIOLOGY

A major concern is the "biology" of an area, that is the numbers of elk and trophy potential. Some elk herds are

You often have to compromise and either choose a high-production area with lots of small bulls, or an area with fewer elk but bigger animals. In regions managed for the maximum number of elk, this 5-point bull would be large. Here Rich LaRocco (left) and Gary Alt estimate the measurements of Rich's bull. It scored 230.

managed for maximum numbers and others are regulated for better trophy hunting. Most high-production herds produce few big bulls, and most good trophy areas either have lower densities of elk, they're inaccessible and tough to hunt, or hunting permits there are limited. In most cases, then, you have to compromise and choose an area with lots of elk and smaller bulls, or one with larger bulls but where the hunting will be tougher.

A good example exists in Colorado. Perhaps the most famous elk herd in the world exists on the White River National Forest near Meeker. The Division of Wildlife estimates this herd at more than 17,000 animals. Hunting success here is high, but following the general rifle season the ratio of bulls to cows is only about 5 bulls/100 cows, which means a high percentage of bulls gets killed each year. Because of the rapid turnover of animals, few bulls survive to old age and trophy-hunting potential is low.

In contrast, wilderness ranges in central Colorado have

ratios of 30 bulls/100 cows and higher, which indicates a good carryover of older bulls fron year to year, but here elk densities are lower and the country is very rugged and inaccessible. In other words animals are tough to hunt, but the trophy potential is much higher.

Similar contrasting conditions exist in all elk states, so to assess the biology of a herd you want to ask about the level of hunting success, elk densities, and bull-cow ratios. Generally the higher the bull/cow ratio,the better the trophy hunting; 30 bulls/100 cows is considered high. Then choose the type of situation that best suits your needs.

In addition to biologists, ask hunters, loggers, and foresters about their observations. Their judgments are subjective and depend not only on the numbers of elk but on their ability to observe. But if a hunter tells you he's heard 10 bulls bugling on one ridge, or a logger says he regularly sees 50 elk on his way to work, you can compare those observations with other data to draw some conclusions.

HUNTABILITY

Along with biology, huntability should influence your planning. Given equal numbers of elk, two areas may prove far different in terms of hunting quality. Here's an example. In consecutive years I hunted Colorado and Montana. The hunting in Colorado was far easier. Friends and I hunted at timberline in relatively open timber, and in a period of 10 days we called in a dozen bulls and had clear shots at all but one. In Montana, a friend and I hunted a low-elevation drainage clogged with jungle-like vegetation. Without question there were more and bigger bulls there than in Colorado. In 10 days we bugled 20 bulls within bow range, several closer than 10 yards, yet I had only one clear shot at a bull. Even though the biology was superior in Montana, the huntability was much higher in Colorado, and killing a bull there was easier.

To assess huntability, ask your sources to paint a picture of vegetation. Topographic maps represent trees with green, but they don't tell the nature of those trees, so ask if they're dense spruce, aspens, open ponderosa pine, juniper, lodgepole pine and so forth.

And have sources characterize the terrain. Tight contour

Tight contour lines on a map could simply indicate steep but easy-to-hike tundra, such as this mountain range west of Denver, Colorado.

lines obviously mean steep country, but what kind of steep? Do those contour lines represent boulder slides and impassible granite cliffs, or do they indicate steep but easy-to-hike tundra?

Part of huntability is picking country that suits your hunting style. Elk country varies from timberline tundra, to black spruce forests, to lodgepole pine flats, to stark granite peaks linked by pockets of fir timber, to juniper and pinion pine, to sagebrush and aspen. There's no "average" elk country. Have sources depict in detail the nature of their regions, and pick those localities that best suit your style of hunting and your esthetic eye.

Also investigate access. In hunting I want to escape from other people, so my idea of good access is no roads or trails. Your idea of good access may be lots of roads and jeep trails. Whatever your choice, know what to expect before you set out. And don't trust your maps. In Colorado, two friends and I drove to an area because a Forest Service map showed only main access roads linked together by foot trails. When we arrived we discovered the "trails" were jeep roads, and the territory was crawling with hunters in 4WD rigs. One phone call to the nearest ranger office to update our maps would have spared us that disappointment.

Many states enforce road closures during hunting seasons, gates are locked across private land, boundaries for parks and wilderness areas change, some roads become quagmires during bad weather, and, of course, new roads are always being built. Get a clear picture of access before the hunt.

HOW TO HUNT

The parameters of biology and huntability may tell you which regions to hunt, but they don't necessarily tell you how to hunt one area. Two mountain ranges may have equal numbers of elk, but in one range, the animals might concentrate at timberline where grasses and feed are best, and in an adjacent range, where meadows and aspen are scattered throughout lower timber, the majority of elk may summer at much lower elevations. Find out the kinds of feeds elk utilize in that region and at what elevations they'll be living during the early season. Also, ask about new burns, logging operations or natural disturbances (remember Mt. St. Helens?) that might attract or disperse animals.

During the early season major migrations from summer to winter range aren't a concern, but on the short term elk may shift locations in response to changing conditions. Find out how weather, such as drought, early frosts, or unseasonable snow; or hunting pressure might influence elk.

The presence of livestock could be significant. Sheep and cattle graze many National Forest and BLM lands. Elk avoid concentrations of domestic stock, and livestock certainly can make stalking difficult, so find out what the situation will be where you plan to hunt.

TIMING

Most early elk seasons extend for a month or more. Should you hunt early or late?

Speaking broadly, elk bugle throughout September, but in some regions, bulls start bugling in August and in most they bugle into early October. Traditional thinking says that the rut peaks in late September so that's the best time to hunt.

That may or may not be true.

For one thing, the rut doesn't necessarily peak in late September. Rut timing is related to the timing of calf drop in the spring; in some regions, depending on prevailing conditions there, calves are born early in the spring, and in other regions they're born later, and the rut varies accordingly. Latitude has little bearing on timing. If anything the rut will come later at northern latitudes because the calving period will fall later in the spring. Learn the specifics of this timing for each region by talking to locals.

Also, consider that the peak of rut may not be the best time to hunt. In terms of bugling bulls within easy range, I've done best very early in the rut, as early as August. Bulls can be pitifully easy to bugle in then, probably because they're fresh and full of energy. They haven't established a pecking order yet, and because they haven't acquired harems, they're roaming, looking for cows. In many cases early-season bulls don't bugle a lot; they seem to come to a call out of curiosity, but they come eagerly. Also, early in the rut bulls haven't had much contact with hunters and aren't as likely to be call shy as they might be later.

The peak of the rut, when bulls are going wild, smashing up trees and bugling and chasing cows constantly can be a more exciting time to hunt, but bugling in a bull can be tougher then. Big bulls have claimed harems, and other bulls are hanging around these herds, trying to get a cut of the action. The order of things is pretty well set, and bulls are getting run down. Many simply don't respond to a call as eagerly as they did earlier.

OTHER CONSIDERATIONS

One thing you might want to investigate is the potential for a combination deer-elk hunt. In some areas that's feasible, but most good elk country does not hold a lot of deer and vice versa. Explore this potential thoroughly before you get your hopes too high.

Plan for meat care. Air temperatures could drop to freezing every night and you'll have no problems just hanging meat in camp, but often that's not the case during early season, so plan ahead. If you're going into backcountry on foot, prearrange for a packer with horses or mules to pack

In some areas a combination hunt for deer and elk is feasible, but don't get your hopes too high. Generally good elk country is not good deer country. Larry Jones (left) killed this buck on an elk hunt in Oregon. I'm giving advice.

meat out for you. Packers aren't available in all areas, so don't wait until you get meat on the ground to think about it. And line up cold storage. If you shoot a bull the first day and have to wait for your buddies to finish out the hunt, you must get that meat on ice. Line up cold storage before the hunt. Most sizeable towns have a Chamber of Commerce that will give you the names of local meat plants.

Maps show the locations of most developed campsites, but they say little about quality. I've failed to inquire ahead of time and have found myself in dry camps. One spot in Colorado had plenty of springs, but cattle had turned them all into muck holes; in Montana my map showed a major creek, but the crazy thing ran underground for miles. Before picking a campsite ask about water availability and quality, flat ground, restrictions on camping and so forth.

Other aspects of hunting such as esthetics, availability of small game, motels and other luxuries may be important to you, so add these to your personal list of research items.

Planning a self-guided hunt takes time and thought, but by doing your homework you're almost guaranteed of enjoying the early-season hunt of a lifetime.

If you're strictly after a trophy bull look for a region with a high bull-cow ratio. Outfitter Ed McCallum is shown with a better-than-average 6-point killed in Idaho's Chamberlain Basin. This bull scores about 300.

Scouting

The Wallowa Mountains of Oregon are big, bad country, tough on a hunter's body and mind. They're also good elk country. That's why we'd had a packer there set up a camp for us 17 miles from the nearest road. One afternoon we sat in camp working on equipment, trimming meat and resting when a bowhunter walked up. He was tall and lean with dark wavy hair held back by a leather band. His eyes were deep brown and searching. His name was Fred. He'd driven all the way from California to hunt here because he loved wilderness. For nine days he'd hunted alone and had loved every minute of it.

There was only one problem—in those nine days he hadn't seen any elk. Not one. It seemed impossible that a person could roam here that long without blundering into one animal along the line. Talking to him, we realized he had no idea about the nature of elk. He'd been hunting above timberline and on south slopes amid magnificent yellow pine and sparse aspen, the most beautiful country he could find. Because he'd seen lots of deer there he assumed that's where he'd find elk, too.

We told Fred what we knew about elk and pointed out some drainages where we'd seen animals in the past. Then Fred drifted out of camp as silently as he'd drifted in.

A few days later he came back. Ecstatic! The very next day he'd gotten into a herd of 11 elk, and he'd seen animals every day since talking to us.

It's one thing to locate a region with lots of elk and another thing to find animals once you get there. That's where scouting comes in. Scouting could be called the link between planning a hunt and locating a bull. It not only helps you to learn where elk are living, but it helps you to learn the country, too.

THE NEEDS OF ELK

Elk are big, heavy-bodied animals with thick hides and dense hair, so getting enough to eat and keeping cool are major concerns in September. In a nutshell, to find elk you look for lush feed, moisture and cool timber. As I've said earlier, the character of elk country varies greatly from region to region, but wherever elk are found, most of them will be concentrated in habitat that provides these qualities.

Hunters often ask: Are elk grazers or browsers? The answer is "Yes." Biologists say that an elk's stomach is more like that of a cow (grazer) than that of a deer (browser), so if grass is abundant, that's what elk feed on most heavily. In any new region I first look for lush meadows, especially wet meadows where springs ooze from the ground and grass is succulent. Boggy meadows consistently attract elk, not only for feed but for wallowing, too. I'll say more about wallows later.

In regions where grass is scarce, elk browse heavily on woody plants. In northwest Montana and north Idaho, for example, dense forests blanket many mountain ranges, and there you'd be hard pressed to find a meadow of any size. In places like this look for patches of alder, willow, huckleberry and hardwoods, or spots where clearcuts, burns, avalanches, boulder slides and other forces break up ceaseless conifer forests and allow shrubs and weeds to grow. Elk will feed in these places.

BEDDING SITES

Breaks in topography might tell you where elk bed. Some elk country is very steep, so animals there will bed on benches or knolls where the terrain levels out. Research has shown that elk like fairly steep grades, from 15 to 40 percent, so in flat country look for bedding sites in canyons and on ridges.

Elk will lie up in any timber that provides cool shade, but consistently you'll find them in pockets of mature, old-growth trees where branches form a dense canopy that shades out second-growth trees and underbrush. Often you can spot these stands from far off, which gives you a clue about where to start hunting.

The presence of water generally characterizes elk habitat. Most northern forests are well watered with rivers and streams, and elk drink from these in passing, but I've rarely found herds living near rushing water, probably because the constant splashing nullifies their sense of hearing. Consistently they feed and bed around seeping springs in dank, cool, silent, dungeon-like surroundings. Draws, depressions, swales, and heads of drainages where springs seep and ooze from the ground will attract and hold herds of elk. You can pick out many of these places from a distance by the appearance of the terrain and by the presence of moisture-loving plants such as alder, willow, spruce or yew.

KEY LOCATIONS

In much elk country you'll find feed, moisture and cover mixed together. Timberline basins and alpine bowls are ideal places to look for and bugle for elk. Timbered east and north-facing slopes consistently attract elk, too, because these aspects get little sun and are cool, moist and lush. Elk can feed, water and bed there without exposing themselves to direct sunlight, which seems to suit them just fine.

That doesn't mean animals don't live on south-facing slopes. One place I call Bull Basin lies on a dry south slope. There, a steep ravine slashes the barren, granite canyonside and springs bubble from the sides of this ravine. Lush meadows flourish near the springs and dense shadowy thickets of spruce flank the meadows. I've always found elk there. Any locale with good feed, water and shade will attract and hold elk. It's just that these qualities most commonly exist in high basins and on north slopes.

In dry regions you may not find a mix of ideal conditions.

Shari Fraker, a Colorado bowhunter, attributes much of her success to scouting. From field observations she creates detailed maps that help her to hunt effectively. This bull, taken in 1982, is one of five elk Fraker has killed in five consecutive years.

In Arizona, for example, elk country along the Mogollon Rim is very dry. Mike Cupell, an authority on elk hunting, said that bulls rarely wallow in Arizona although they may roll in the dust. Reservoirs, stock tanks, and tiny seep springs supply the only water, and elk are dependent on these for drinking. In this country elk commonly travel five miles or more each day from water and feed to bedding ridges. Experienced hunters know the locations of all water sources, and they either hunt from stands there, or they use waterholes as starting points for further scouting to determine the daily movement patterns of elk.

ELK MOVEMENTS

As you're scouting, of course, you're always looking for elk and for fresh sign. Don't expect to find animals in every good spot, because even the best places will be empty at times, but if you've looked over miles of ideal habitat and haven't found evidence of elk, try to figure out why.

Elk move rapidly in response to immediate conditions. A Colorado biologist said that in the South Gore Range, elk generally summer at timberline, at an elevation of 11,000 feet, but if frosts in late August or early September burn grasses there, animals may drop 2,000 feet or more in elevation to locate green succulent feed. That's consistent with the observations of Shari Fraker, a Colorado bowhunter who's spent hundreds of hours scouting and studying elk year -round. Fraker said she thinks elk follow a "green line." That is, in spring they move up as the snow retreats, staying right at the leading edge of greenup. In fall they do the reverse, moving down to find green feed just below the frost line.

A sudden snowstorm can move elk around. I've been hit by heavy snow several times in late September, and it has always taken me some time to relocate them. Hunting one year at 11,600 feet elevation, Fraker got hit by a storm that dumped four inches of snow. She dropped down to an alternate area at 10,000 feet. Just before midnight that night the constant bugling of bulls around camp woke her up, and she believes that the snow higher up pushed the elk down.

Dry conditions definitely affect elk. In northeast Oregon my friends and I couldn't find animals on traditionally good

Your time is well spent sitting on vantage points, using binoculars to study the country intensively. From places like this you can spot breaks in terrain and vegetation that will attract elk.

In a nutshell, to find elk you look for lush feed, moisture and cool timber. The basin pictured here has lush meadows at the bottom of the draw, where elk feed and wallow in cool mud, surrounded by shadowy thickets of spruce, where elk can bed in comfort. This habitat is perfect for elk.

north slopes, so we looked around and located major herds on an unlikely dry south slope. That seemed especially odd since it was a drought year, but that fact may have explained the situation. No rain had fallen all summer, so even north slopes had dried up. Patches of alder provided about the only green feed, and most alders grew in avalanche chutes on south slopes, so that's where elk had concentrated.

In Montana, bowhunter Ron Granneman hunts the same general areas year after year. He said that one of his favorite areas has excellent habitat but in dry years, elk simply don't use it.

Elk are sensitive to disturbance, and within a given area they'll gravitate to the most peaceful conditions they can find, so consider that in scouting. In deep wilderness where people are scarce that may not be a serious thought, but in accessible regions where roads give hunters good access, where logging, grazing, backpacking, fishing or other recreation take place, elk will congregate in pockets of refuge. That could mean simply one drainage or canyon without road access, or where even that's not available, it might mean sanctuaries of the densest, nastiest brush and timber around.

SCOUTING METHODS

Knowing what to look for is one thing, but knowing **how** to look is another. Here are some ideas.

One time a friend and I waited too long to order topographic maps; they didn't arrive before the hunt so we went without. Our National Forest maps showed roads and access, which was a good start, but without topographic maps to show terrain details we felt helpless. I'd as soon leave my elk call home as to hunt without topographic maps.

You can virtually scout most elk country by studying contour lines and colorations on maps. Topo maps clearly show basins, draws, benches, saddles, meadows, ridges, north slopes, moist areas and springs—most of the variations and features that will attract and hold elk.

Here's an example. Gary Alt and I had futilely combed miles of timber. It seemed barren. There was very little feed and we'd found no fresh sign. Then as we stomped back toward camp one evening we heard a bull bugle. We investigated to find a small, lush meadow, like an oasis in the middle of a desert, and the place was rank with sign. The bull obviously had lived there a long time. Later I looked at a topographic map. Sure enough, right there contour lines on the map bulged slightly, indicating a flat spot, and white speck amid green on the map indicated an opening. If we'd read our map carefully to start with we could have picked that meadow out beforehand and saved ourselves plenty of effort.

DRIVING

Driving roads may be a poor way to hunt elk, but it's a good way to scout. In backcountry you can't scout by driving, of course, but where roads exist, you must know the road systems to hunt efficiently. Even if you come into a new area during the season, I'd suggest you sacrifice at least one day just to drive roads and jeep trails to get a feel for the land and the access. That knowledge will save you hours of valuable time as you're hunting.

Jay Elmer, who killed Pope and Young world record elk in two consecutive years, purposely stays out of the woods before the season to avoid spooking elk, so he scouts by driving. Jay prescouts with maps to pick out waterholes and potential bedding ridges. Then he drives his area to assess the vegetation and to search for elk tracks and trails. In his part of Arizona roads crisscross the country, so traveling elk must cross roads somewhere. Jay's purpose is to familiarize himself with the country, to learn the lay of hills and canyons, to locate good bedding and feeding sites, and to study movement patterns of animals. He pieces extensive observations together like a puzzle to form a picture that leads to a hunting strategy.

VANTAGE POINTS

In flat or rolling country it's hard to get an overview short of renting an airplane, but in steep mountains you can locate points, ridges, hilltops, fire towers and other viewpoints. Your time is well spent sitting on these places, using binoculars to study the country intensively. Just as you can pick out topography on a map, you can pinpoint elky terrain and vegetation with on-the-ground observation. Looking across a canyon, for example, you can pick out benches and basins, the heads of drainages, meadows, willow patches, old-growth timber, and so forth.That's equally as revealing as flying over the country, and it's a lot cheaper.

From these same spots, look for animals. Elk don't like direct sunlight, so you have to watch before sunrise or after sunset, or on heavily overcast days.

SCOUTING ON FOOT

Many hunters debate the value of scouting on foot. Some say that the purpose of scouting is to learn the country, not to see elk. On the other hand, how do you evaluate sign if you don't get out there and look around? By scouting on foot ahead of the season, you could spook animals and nullify your very reasons for scouting. That's not as serious with Roosevelt elk, which live in the dense coastal mountains of Oregon and Washington, because they remain in a fairly confined territory, but disturbed Rocky Mountain elk may take off and set up housekeeping miles away, and you'll have to start all over locating a herd. Of course, if the season is open, you'll probably just combine scouting with hunting.

Shari Fraker, who has killed elk during five consecutive seasons, believes in scouting on foot to learn as much as possible about the elk in her part of Colorado, but to avoid disturbing animals, she scouts in full camouflage, keeps the wind in her favor and never walks into the open. She tries to remain inconspicuous, strictly an unseen observer.

SIGN

Evaluating sign is a big part of hunting, but it applies to scouting, too. If you've never hunted elk before you might wonder what elk tracks look like, and I'd say they look like small cattle tracks. Tracks of bulls are rounded and blunt much like those of domestic bulls, and they may be up to 4-1 inches long. Tracks of cows are smaller and slightly more pointed, somewhat like oversized deer tracks.

Elk travel long distances with ease, and you'll find single tracks crossing high saddles or divides or passing through barren timber. These desultory tracks tell you only that an

Rub trees are always exciting finds because they tell you a bull or bulls have been in the area. Here Gary Alt looks at a rubbed aspen tree in Colorado.

Elk wallows are bathtub-sized depressions in the mud. You'll find them frequently in boggy meadows. You can tell the wallow Rich LaRocco has found in Colorado isn't real fresh because the water has begun to clear.

elk has passed by. Concentrated tracks on well-used trails or around meadows and brush patches mean you'd better get serious. A herd is hanging out in that area. Judge the age of the tracks. If the edges are sharp and the tracks aren't eroded by frost, wind or rain, rest assured you're very close to some elk.

Elk feeding primarily on grass or other soft plants will leave droppings much like miniature cow pies, and animals feeding on woody browse drop pellets. If droppings are green and shiny you know they're very fresh, and even if they've turned black but are still moist and green inside, they're no more than a few days old. Most elk pellets are about the size of black olives, and at one time I thought pellet size told something about animal size. Then I killed a large bull in Idaho and its pellets were smaller than peas. If I'd seen them on the ground, I'd have said they'd come from a small deer.

Smell is valid elk sign. The animals themselves smell as strong as barnyard cattle, and their urine is powerful, too. If you suddenly think you smell horses or cattle, assume you're smelling a herd of elk or at least elk beds, and investigate thoroughly.

Rub trees are always exciting finds. In late summer bulls rub the velvet off their antlers and later, when the rut starts, they tear up trees with their antlers in mock battles. In the wake of these activities they leave dozens of trees with the bark shredded off. Rub trees. Fresh rubs may be of greatest immediate interest, but take note of all rubs. Ron Granneman said that elk have traditional rutting grounds. Old rubs dating back 5 to 10 years could indicate a traditional rutting ground, which probably will be a consistently good area to hunt.

Elk wallows are bathtub-sized depressions in mud. You'll find them in soft meadows or in the mud of oozing springs in dark timber. Elk wallow in hot weathear to cool off, and apparently they wallow as part of the rutting ritual. Biologists say bull elk try to demonstrate dominance through bugling, aggressive actions, appearance and smell. During the rut a bull's neck swells considerably and he develops a huge shaggy mane, which are physiological changes to make the bull look big and mean. Apparently wallowing contributes by adding a crusty layer of foul-smelling mud. If water in a wallow is still murky and you can clearly see impressions of hair in mud around the edges, you know it's fresh, and that a bull is lurking somewhere close by.

PULLING IT ALL TOGETHER

Scouting can yield an invaluable storehouse of information. Make notes on your observations, and use your findings to develop detailed maps. Shari Fraker scouts extensively and records all of her findings on topographic maps. She codes all hills with the letters A,B,C,D; notes the times at which she sees animals in particular areas; charts out their travel routes; draws in wallows and rub-tree locations; marks bedding sites and so forth. She constructs an accurate picture of her country, so when it comes time to hunt she makes no false moves, wastes no precious hunting time stumbling around elkless country. You may not have the opportunity to scout and study elk the way Fraker does, but with the right approach you can learn a lot about your elk country in a short period. And then you're ready to locate a bull.

Calls and Calling

Hunter's opinions about bugling run to the extremes. On the one hand, really good buglers, those who bugle in not only elk but other hunters, too, are revered as if they possess supernatural ability. Beginners stand in awe and think they have to bugle just like that to **ever** coax a bull elk within range. Indeed most bulls can distinguish blatant phonies from the real thing, but they're not magicians and they can be fooled, so don't throw in the towel just because you're not the greatest. I'm only an average bugler, but I've enjoyed some remarkable experiences with elk.

On the other hand, don't slough off learning to bugle. Bugling ability will make a difference—a big difference—in your success. So rife are stories about how a fiery-eyed bull tried to make love to the outfitter's horse or how the steely-eyed guide whistled through his teeth and brought a bull on the run,that uninitiatedhunters assume that crazed, rutting bulls will attack without provocation. Indeed an occasional bull goes off the deep end and does something stupid, but you'll have a lot of dry seasons if you entrust your success to that hope alone.

CALLING DOES MAKE A DIFFERENCE

Most experienced elk hunters agree on the importance of bugling quality. Ron Granneman said that before the grunt

Mike Schlegel of Idaho is one hunter who thinks that bugling ability makes a great deal of difference in elk hunting. Schlegel uses his voice to produce a variety of elk-like sounds. This bull, killed by Schlegel in Idaho, scores 343 Pope and Young points. (Photo courtesy Mike Schlegel)

tube came along—I'll say more about grunt tubes later—he used only the traditional elk whistle. Rarely did he call in a bull, and elk so frequently shut up when he bugled that he decided bulls really didn't want anything to do with each other. Since he's perfected voice bugling with the aid of a grunt tube, he's found that bulls definitely will come to his calling. Granneman thinks calling ability makes the difference between bugling in two to three bulls a season and 15 to 20.

Mike Schlegel, a well-known elk hunter and biologist in Idaho, agrees. As a typical example, he said one time he could hear three bulls around him. Several times he blew a commercial call and none of the bulls ever answered it, but every time he bugled with his voice, which sounds very much like an elk, the bulls hollered right back.

Larry Jones, who lives, thinks and sleeps elk hunting, bugled in his share of bulls using a traditional elk whistle, but he wasn't satisfied with that, so he developed a bugle with a

The Larry D. Jones elk call uses a stainless-steel reed to produce its realistic elk-like sound. The plastic reed head detaches quickly so that the flexible pipe can be used as a grunt tube.

metal reed attached to a grunt tube. It has a realistic "bull" sound. Over a given amount of time, he has called in about three times as many bulls with that as he did with a whistle.

My experience is very similar. Without question, the more you sound like an elk, the more bulls you're going to fool.

GOOD CALLING

What is "good" calling? The traditional whistle, which is made from straight plastic pipe, rubber hose, or copper tubing, sounds like a whistle and lacks the flute-like resonance of most bulls. Any experienced elk hunter can distinguish a whistle from an elk at long range because the quality of sound is different. If hunters can distinguish that, most elk probably can, too.

In addition, whistles lack variation. Each time you blow, they sound the same, and that's a problem. For one thing, no two bulls sound exactly alike. The "typical" elk bugle starts with a low note, ascends through several octaves like a calliope to hit a shrill high note, then descends the scale and ends with grunting, chuckling and braying sounds. But that pattern has hundreds of nuances. In Montana Larry Jones and I about split our sides laughing about "The Screamer," a bull that sounded like someone who'd fallen off a cliff and shattered a leg. I dubbed another bull "The Moo Cow" because his strained voice sounded like a Hereford cow bellowing for her lost calf. He never did really bugle.

Also, any one bull will produce a variety of shrills, squeals, grunts, brays and chuckles, and it's important to get this variety into your calling. One time a friend worked on a bull as I listened from a nearby hillside. It was like a running battle and I measured their progress by sound. My friend would bugle and the bull would bellow back, and the sounds of antlers clattering on limbs echoed through the trees. Gradually their bugling came closer together, but then they seemed to reach a stalemate. They came no closer and at dark my friend emerged from the woods.

"The bull was coming good," he said. "But when he got within 50 yards he hung up and wouldn't come any closer."

Listening to this battle, I'd noticed one thing—my friend's bugling always sounded the same. His call produced realistic ascending-descending bugle notes, but the pattern never varied. I couldn't help but think that the monotony of his calling made the bull suspicious.

VARIETY IS IMPORTANT

Or maybe the repetitious bugling simply didn't strike a responsive cord in the bull. In preparing his beautiful book SEASON OF THE ELK (Lowell Press, Kansas City, MO), Dean Krakel II listened to hundreds of elk and recorded their bugling on tape, and he observed their rutting and fighting. He writes, "Just as bulls bugle in a variety and combination of sounds ranging from grunts, whistles, barks, screams, whines, moans and roars, they also bugle for many different reasons.... In the course of my field work, I have recorded some ninety minutes of elk bugles. I have played the tapes back to a variety of bulls, sometimes using their own voices. Often, a bull will graze while the recording plays. Then suddenly a certain tone, a certain pattern of bugling evokes instantaneous anger.... The same recording will evoke dif-

Whistles made out of a straight piece of pipe or hose are traditional in elk hunting. They're loud and durable, but they lack the realistic sound produced by other calls.

ferent responses from different bulls. A small bull will slink away. A larger bull will bugle back.''

Apparently there's no precise prescription of sounds to incite violence from a bull. As Krakel said, it may depend on which bull you're talking to. So a good approach is to arm yourself with a variety of elk talk and experiment on each bull until you find the one that works. Mike Schlegel, using his voice, produces a half-dozen bugles, grunts and squeals, and he mixes up these sounds in various combinations until he hits on the one that antagonizes a bull.

Ron Granneman said he carries three bugles taped together—a long-range whistle, a bugle made of spiraled gas pipe, and a grunt tube. He'll first try one and then another until one produces a good heated response from a bull.

Larry Jones uses a similar approach. He bugles with a metal-reed call, a diaphragm that fits in his mouth, and his voice. In addition, as most hunters do, he ''calls'' by beating and raking on limbs with a stick to simulate the sound of a bull tearing up a tree with its antlers. While working on one bull, Larry might bugle with any one or all of his calls, and

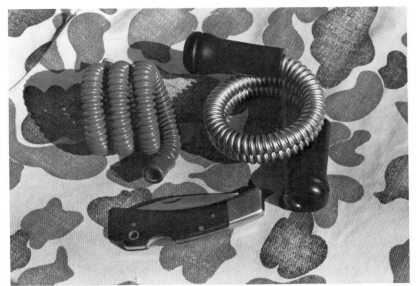

Another type of "whistle" is the curly-cue bugle, which is basically a coiled section of gas pipe. The bugle on the left is distributed by Martin Archery and the other is made by Scotch Game Calls.

he'll mix in some raking. If that doesn't work, he might quit bugling altogether and just rake a tree. In other words, he experiments until he figures out what really rankles a bull.

GETTING THE PITCH

Obviously I can't describe on paper what a bull sounds like. You have three options for learning bull sounds: Listen to live bulls, have an experienced hunter demonstrate, or buy a record or tape with recorded bugling. Many companies sell instructional tapes (I've listed several in Appendix B). Listen to one of these recordings and mimic what you hear.

Many hunters say they can tell the difference between big bulls and little bulls by the sounds of their bugling. Big, old bulls have gruff, deep, resonant voices with lots of grunts and coughs, they say, but young bulls have squeaky, high-pitched voices. They conclude that the idea behind bugling is to sound like a squeaky little bull. They reason that no bull wants to tangle with a bull bigger than himself, so if you sound big and

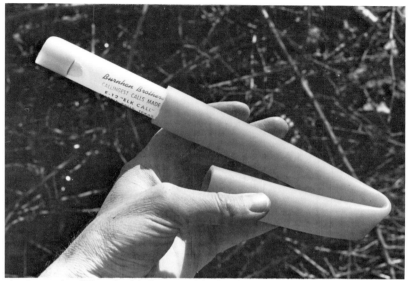
As far as traditional whistles go, this flexible call was made by Burnham Brothers is a good choice.

bad you'll run off little bulls, but if you sound squeaky and little, bigger bulls will be eager to come in and whip your tail.

I don't buy that. First, that reasoning assumes that two bulls always come together to fight, but experienced observers say that bulls rarely fight; normally they just thrash trees with their antlers and bugle and strut, trying to intimidate each other, but that's all. Also, any bull wants to do his share of the breeding, so it seems reasonable that a small bull without a harem might eagerly come to the sound of a big bull that probably has receptive cows in his presence. Finally, bulls often seem to approach out of curiosity. Many times I've been bugling, sounding as big, bad and mean as possible, and have had bulls ranging in size from small to huge, walk in silently, never bugling at all, seemingly more curious than belligerent. That's been particularly true early in the rut.

Second, the sound of a bull's bugling may not reflect his size at all. Some hunters say they can distinguish big and little bulls, but I have my doubts. You know as well as I do that in barbershop quartets the football lineman always sings tenor and the 118-pound weakling sings bass. In other words, there's no correlation between size and voice quality. It may be irrelevant anthropomorphism to relate humans to animals, but I suspect the same principle applies to most animals, including elk.

Again quoting Dean Krakel: "A bull's age does not determine the sound of his bugle. Even in early fall, before constant bugling makes voices hoarse, I have heard the oldest, largest bulls emit only scratchy, high-pitched squeaks, while the youngest, scrawniest juveniles sound forth in mellow, full-bodied tones that would put a concert flutist to shame."

One day my friend Larry Jones worked on a bull for an hour or more, getting more and more excited as the bull bellowed powerfully and grunted and chirped. Judging from the sound of this beast, Larry knew he had a world-record bull on the line.

"What a disappointment when a dinky—and I mean dinky—little 4-point walked into view," Larry said.

CHOOSING A BUGLE

Calls fall into three general categories: Whistle, reed and diaphragm. As I've said, whistles made out of a straight piece of pipe or hose are traditional. Many hunters use them today and they do work, but new better variations have evolved. The Challenger Elk Bugle made by Glenn Jones of Idaho incorporates a plastic whistle with a flexible hose, which increases resonance and quality of the whistle sound. Also, you can separate the whistle and hose to use the hose as a grunt tube for voice bugling.

Another type of whistle is the "curly-cue" bugle, which is basically a section of twisted gas pipe. This call produces an excellent series of breaking, flute-like sounds and it's easy to blow, but it doesn't produce a great variety of sounds.

The only reed-type elk bugle I've seen is made by Larry D. Jones of Oregon. A plastic head houses a durable metal reed, and that's connected to an 18-inch grunt tube. The reed head and tube can be disconnected with a quick twist to give you a straight grunt tube. This bugle produces a realistic calliope sound and is easy to use.

Diaphragm calls come in two styles: Mouth and external. Mouth diaphragms originated as turkey calls, but they're

RATINGS: good average poor	DURABILITY	EASE OF USE	REALISTIC SOUND	VARIETY OF SOUNDS	LOUDNESS
TRADITIONAL WHISTLE	good	good	poor	poor	good
CHALLENGER ELK BUGLE	average	good	average	average	good
"CURLY CUE" WHISTLE	good	good	average	average	average
LARRY D. JONES BUGLE (metal reed)	good	good	good	average	good
MOUTH DIAPHRAGM	poor	poor	good	good	good
EXTERNAL DIAPHRAGM (Old Jake Products)	poor	average	good	good	good
VOICE	varies with individual	poor	good	good	varies with individual

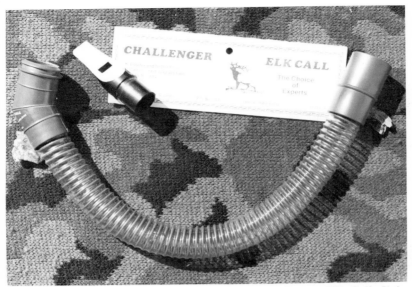

A variation on the traditional whistle is the Challenger Elk Call. It incorporates a plastic whistle with a grunt tube.

fast becoming popular with elk hunters. With them it's possible to produce a variety of squeals and chuckles, and your hands are always free unless you blow through a grunt tube, as many hunters do, to increase resonance. Diaphragms, which are made of thin latex, aren't as durable as whistles and reed calls, and they're harder to master. Some people never seem to get the hang of it.

Here are some tips for blowing a diaphragm call. First, bend and shape the call to conform to the roof of your mouth. It must form a tight seal. To control pitch, increase and decrease tongue pressure against the latex diaphragm. Now, push from way down in your stomach to force air across the diaphragm. Concentrate on pushing air with your stomach; if you focus on the call you'll get all tongue-tied. Mastering these calls takes practice, but they're effective once you do.

Old Jake Products of Vermont makes an exterior diaphragm call, The Imitator, that produces an excellent variety of sounds and is plenty loud, and it's easier to use than mouth diaphragms. The major drawback I've seen is

Old Jake Products of Vermont makes an exterior diaphragm call that produces an excellent variety of sounds. The only drawback is that the thin diaphragm can be damaged easily.

that the diaphragm is fairly fragile. You're wise to carry some spares in case you have a blowout.

VOICE BUGLING

Many hunters use commercial calls in conjunction with their voices. At long range they blow a whistle, reed or diaphragm call to locate a bull, then as they move in they bugle and grunt with their voices. Most voice buglers use a grunt tube to increase the volume and resonance of their voices. Any piece of pipe or tubing 1 to 2 inches in diameter and 15 to 25 inches long makes a good grunt tube. Flexible tubing is easier to carry than a stiff pipe, and corrugated tubing is ideal because it produces realistic breaking notes as you bugle through it.

If you have the vocal cords for it, voice bugling can be the most deadly method because you can produce any number of realistic sounds. The drawbacks are that it takes practice and your throat may give out after a day of bugling. Also, some people just can't do it.

Children and women who have high-pitched voices can bugle by screaming, but most men's voices are too low so they bugle by sucking in. Try it. Expel all the air from your lungs, then pushing with your lower abdomen for power, suck in air to create a whistling sound in your throat. Practice to get the right pitch and to get your throat in shape. You'll get hoarse at first, but with experience you'll develop a convincing line of bull.

RAKING

Feisty bulls often tear into trees and brush with their antlers, and you can hear these mock battles from some distance. Producing similar noises greatly enhances your own bugling efforts. As you bugle, use a limb 2 to 3 inches in diameter to beat on branches and scrape bark off a tree trunk. Bulls often clatter their antlers violently against a tree for 5 to 10 seconds, then they'll rub up and down with their brow tines, peeling bark off a tree, which produces methodical scraping sounds. Amidst this carrying on they'll bugle and grunt, and at times they'll be absolutely still. Try to reproduce this pace and timing with your raking and bugling. Don't set up a continuous clatter. In some cases you can "rattle" in a bull without bugling at all, and that can be an effective approach in heavily-hunted regions where bulls are getting call shy.

RATING A CALL

What constitutes a good elk bugle? I rate calls in terms of durability, ease of use, realistic sound, variety of sound, and volume. A call has to be reasonably loud, especially for locating bulls at long range. In Appendix B I've listed addresses of call and instructional-tape makers, and I tell how to make your own calls.

Locating a Bull

You've planned, you've scouted, you've learned to bugle. You're ready to hunt. And you'll face probably the most difficult aspect of elk hunting right off. Locating animals.

For the person who's hunted only deer, trying to find elk can be frustrating and bewildering. In good country, deer may be scattered anywhere, so frequently you see animals, or at least fresh sign. But even in the finest areas, elk are distributed spottily, and you may go miles without seeing animals or sign. In general elk are herd animals; they live in bunches and commonly confine their movements to small, separate pockets of ideal habitat. You can walk within 100 yards of a herd of elk yet see no sign of their presence. Within any given drainage, 90 percent of the elk may concentrate on 10 percent of the habitat, and the rest of the drainage is devoid of animals. That's why locating elk calls for a specialized approach.

THE METHOD

You locate elk by bugling. Any hunter who's pursued elk in October or November when the animals are silent knows how crafty and ghost-like elk can be. They seem to disappear into the ground. They're invisible.

For that reason, their bugling in September opens up a whole new world. It allows you to locate animals by sound, which is an inestimable advantage.

Here are the basics of locating early-season bulls. In some cases you may be driving or riding a horse, but in most you'll be walking. You set out early in the morning, hiking a trail or ridgetop, blowing your bugle into basins, meadow areas, alpine bowls, timber pockets and other likely spots. Biologists say that bugling is a form of "advertising" for bulls, and one bull responds to the bugle of another bull because he wants to out-advertise that bull. So generally those within hearing distance will respond to your call with a bugle of their own, and you've accomplished the toughest part of elk hunting. You've located a bull.

The amount you bugle will vary greatly depending on topography. In general I'd bugle every 10 to 15 minutes, but in some areas that might not be enough. It's often said you can hear a bull bugling from a mile away, and on a still morning, listening across a canyon, that might be true, but I've hunted convoluted, brushy country where you couldn't hear a bull from 100 yards. In that kind of terrain I might bugle every 5 minutes, or at least often enough for every bull there to hear my calling before I've walked close enough to spook him.

Don't be afraid to cover some ground. Because elk herds are widely scattered, you'll do no good pussyfooting and sneaking around a canyon unless you have good reason to think elk are there. Just take off fast and keep moving until you find some red-hot sign or hear a bull. That's the time to slow down and get cautious. Serious elk buglers hike anywhere from 5 to 20 miles a day, searching for sign and bugling.

That isn't to suggest that you run rampantly through the woods, going for record distances. Quality mileage is important. The purpose of scouting is to provide a starting point for hunting, and if you've studied maps, driven roads, hiked trails, and looked over your country from every possible angle, you have some idea of where elk are living. Before each hunting day, plan an itinerary that will lead you from one promising locality to another. In parts of Oregon, where I've hunted many times, I can link together a chain of good

Don't be afraid to cover some ground. Elk live in pockets and herds could be separated by several miles. Go hard until you hit fresh sign or hear a bull. That's the time to get cautious. In this country during early season, elk will avoid dry, south slopes; they'll keg up on heavily timbered north slopes.

habitats so I waste very little time wandering around marginal country.

You may be worried about traveling fast and quietly at the same time, but that's no big problem. Elk themselves clomp and bang around, so they pay little attention to the sounds of snapping branches or sliding rocks. Until you've located good sign or heard a bull, concentrate more on covering ground than on moving quietly.

At the same time, don't make human sounds—talking, clanking of bows or rifles, rustling of clothing. That will send elk into flight. And be doubly careful not to be smelled or seen. It should go without saying that you always hunt into the wind; elk have exceptional noses. And stick to timber, out of sight. In my opinion, elk have much better eyesight than deer. If you cross open meadows or rock slides, they'll spot you at long distances and leave the country before you ever get close enough to bugle them.

Along that same line, don't get careless about where you bugle. An elk could be bedded 40 yards away or standing just

One big advantage of hunting during the rut, opposed to late-season hunting, is that you can locate bulls by sound. The basic approach is to hike cross country, blowing your call, until a bull answers you. Here I'm using an Old Jake diaphragm call to try to locate a bull in Montana.

over the crest of a hill, and at the first sound of your bugle he could come running. Take precautions before you bugle. Never stand out in the open and bugle. To be safe, always assume a bull is hanging out nearby and take cover before you sound off. One day, Gary Alt and I foolishly sat on an open cliff and started bugling. We knew elk had gone into the trees below us, but we didn't know exactly where they were; our intention was simply to get a response from the bull so we could pinpoint the herd. We bugled for 10 minutes and got no response so we started to walk down the hill, and a bull bolted from 30 yards away, right below the cliff we'd perched on. He'd never bugled to let us know where he was and we'd unknowingly bugled him in. Whenever you blow that call, be prepared for a bull. You never know when one will pop in without knocking.

GIVE A BULL SOME TIME

Your progress throughout the day will be a matter of stop and go. Indeed you must travel the ground, but you want to give good places the attention they deserve. Hurry through the so-so country, but if you hit fresh sign or come to a prime meadow or bedding area, give the place some time. Bulls don't always answer right away. During the middle of the day, or in hot weather, or if they're tired from rutting all night, bulls may be feeling lazy. If you bugle just once they may not answer, but if you persist, you might get a response.

Gary Alt and I did this late one morning. Hiking a timberline ridge in Colorado, we came to the edge of an alpine cirque. Succulent meadows blanketed the upper end, and they gave way farther down to shadowy spruce timber. It looked like elk paradise, and we expected to get an immediate response. We bugled. No answer. We bugled again. Still no answer. We sat quietly for five minutes and bugled again. Silence.

"There's gotta be an elk down there," I said. "Let's eat a snack and give him some time."

We munched granola bars and bugled every five minutes or so. After a half-hour I was about ready to give up when the faint whistle of a bull rose from the bottom of the cirque. Gary and I hiked down into the basin and called a little 5-point within 35 yards.

In trying to locate a bull, your progress will be stop and go. You'll hurry fast through marginal habitat, but when you hit fresh sign, slow down and bugle out the area thoroughly. Here Larry Jones looks over a freshly used wallow, which tells him a bull is probably within bugling distance. (Photo courtesy Larry D. Jones)

That took place at midday, so it's possible the bull was resting and our persistent calling finally prodded him to answer. Or it could be he was worked up and bugling all along and we just weren't hearing him. Another time Gary and I split up, and I sat on a hillside to bugle as Gary circled below to look for a bull. Over a 20-minute period I bugled a half-dozen times and never heard any response, so I assumed there weren't any bulls around. Then Gary came running up the hill out of breath and excited.

"Man, did you hear that sucker down there?" he whispered, through his panting. "Everytime you blew the call he went nuts, grunting and squealing, and ripping up trees."

Never pass lightly over a good area. Bugle several times. Wait, listen, move quietly to get a new angle and bugle again. You'll be surprised at what you uncover.

MAKE THEM BUGLE!

Remember that the purpose of your calling is to make those bulls bugle. Larry Jones, shown here with one of several bulls he's taken, says you don't wait for bulls to bugle; you make them bugle. (Photo courtesy of Larry D. Jones)

It's worth emphasizing that the purpose of your calling is to solicit a response from a bull. You don't wait for him to bugle on his own; you use your call to make him bugle. My friend Larry Jones consistently creates more elk action than anybody I've hunted with, and he doesn't put himself at the mercy of the elk; he puts them at his mercy.

"You create your own action," Larry said. "If those bulls aren't bugling, you make them bugle!"

And I've seen it work. One blustery day in Montana, Larry and I sat on a vast timbered ridge looking across a canyon. We knew there were elk here, but I'd blown my call a couple of times and hadn't got a response. Larry grabbed my call and said, "Let me try that thing!"

He went berserk, blowing it twice as loud as I had, violent, raspy shrieks that would have put a grizzly bear to flight. And he didn't stop with one. He bugled three times in succession—tweet, tweet, tweet. He'd no sooner finished than a bull opened up across the canyon. Larry bugled right back. Pretty soon another bull joined in. Then another, and another. By the time we decided to go after them, six bulls had started raising Cain over there. I've seen that happen several times. Larry gets the ball rolling, and pretty soon the bulls are bugling at each other.

"Guys seem to be afraid they'll spook animals out of the country, but if you sound anything at all like a bull you won't bother them at that distance," he said. "If bulls aren't bugling, you make them bugle. It's when you get in close that you have to be careful."

OTHER INDICATORS

Bugling is the primary way to locate a bull, but you may hear things other than bugling. One is the clattering of antlers on trees or branches. One time while walking a hillside I heard loud thrashing in the creek bottom below. To me it sounded like cattle stumbling around in an aspen grove, so I hurried on to get away from the disturbance. Fortunately for me a bull bugled down there before I got out of hearing. That clattering hadn't been cattle at all but a dandy 6-point bull working himself up for a fight. I'd heard that antler clattering at least 10 minutes before he bugled.

As I've said under "Scouting," you can smell elk from a long way, so always be using your nose. And take time to spot elk at long distances, too. In the mountains west of Denver, friends and I hurried to timberline before daylight each morning, and right at dawn we often spotted elk grazing on the open tundra. By sunup the animals would disappear into timber to bed for the day, but by observing we at least had an idea of where they'd gone and where to begin our bugling. I've had similar success spotting elk in Oregon. In one mountain range, avalanche chutes filled with alder trees slash through the dense forests. On many cool, cloudy afternoons, I've spotted elk feeding in these small openings. I think binoculars are essential for locating elk. I always carry my 7x35 Bausch & Lomb binoculars around my neck. They're held in place by an elastic band around my chest.

PRIME TIMES

As in most types of hunting, early and late in the day are

In the mountains west of Denver, friends and I hurried to timberline before daylight each morning, and right at dawn we often spotted elk grazing on the open tundra. Always carry and use binoculars when you're hunting elk.

the best times to bugle elk. In many cases, bulls rut all night long. One year I shot an elk right at dark and spent much of the night dressing the animal. Just at dark a bull started bugling above me and two others called from across the canyon. They bugled continuously until midnight, then quit. At 4 a.m. they started again and went hot and heavy until about 7 a.m. That pattern is fairly typical, so to hit the peak of morning activity, you should be hiking well before daylight to arrive at your hunting grounds at first light before bulls wind down for the day. That first hour of daylight is an excellent time to locate a bull.

Late evening may be even better. By morning, most bulls are fatigued from rutting throughout the night. They're tired and may not respond eagerly to your bugling. But by evening—under normal circumstances—they're rested up from a day of lying around, and they're ready to begin another night of carousing. That's when they're most aggressive and eager to respond, so evening may be the best time to locate and bugle in a bull. Plan a hunting day so you'll hit prime areas during those choice last few minutes of daylight.

That requires planning and special equipment. For the bowhunter particularly, who often has to trail an animal after a hit, a good flashlight is mandatory. Also, survival gear should always be part of your daily hunting gear in case you get caught out after dark and can't make it back to camp.

You can't hunt at night, of course, but you certainly can locate elk then. Mike Cupell, an excellent elk hunter, said that in Arizona, days generally get so warm that elk brush up and rarely respond to a call. To locate bulls early and to get in a good morning's hunt, Cupell starts bugling at 2 a.m. He normally has a bull located before daylight so that he can get right after the bull by dawn.

Cupell's approach of bugling in the dark can be used to locate bulls anywhere. You can hike trails or drive roads at night, stopping to bugle regularly, and you'll often get more responses than you would during the day. Once you've heard a bull, mark his location as best you can and return the next day to hunt him. You'll probably find the animal in the same general area.

LOCATING A BULL AT MIDDAY

Night and its grey edges of dawn and dusk may be the ideal times to locate a bull, but in most regions, unless the weather is stifling, you can locate bulls all day. Let's face it, most of us travel a long way from home to hunt elk. We want to make the most of our time, and because we don't know exactly where elk are located, we may spend a half-day just finding a spot that holds elk. For those reasons we bugle and hunt all day long.

I think the chances of locating a bull by bugling are almost as good at midday as they are early and late. In Colorado two friends and I bugled ten bulls within bow range. Two were located before 8 a.m.; one after 6 p.m.; and the other seven were located and bugled in between 10 a.m. and 1 p.m. In the Chamberlain Basin of Idaho, I killed a bull that started bugling right at noon and came into my call at 1 o'clock on a sunny afternoon.

WEATHER

Weather may affect your hunting, but again, most of us

Dark, gloomy days are ideal for elk hunting. Under these conditions animals may stay active and in the open all day long. Never waste an overcast day by sitting in camp. That's the time to put in the mileage.

will hunt all day regardless of the weather. With their heavy bodies and thick, insulating hides, elk seem to abhor heat and direct sunlight. That's why they're most active at night and in the morning and evening, but they'll be just as active at other times if conditions are cool. I've enjoyed some of my best action on dark, cloudy, drizzly days, the kind of days I longed to be sitting by a warm campfire, telling elk hunting stories. One afternoon in Oregon, storms marched over the Blue Mountains like brigades of soldiers, drenching the mountains with one shower after another. Randy Bryan and I sat out the heavy rains, then worked on the elk that seemed to be everywhere. At 2 p.m. we watched 20 elk lying in an open meadow. There were six bulls, and a fine herd bull was ripping and tearing all afternoon, right out in the open. That would be a rare sight on a sunny day. At 11 a.m. under a steady drizzle in Montana, I could hear at least six bulls calling back and forth, and I hadn't even bugled; they were just naturally active in that cool weather. Never waste a dark, overcast day by sitting in camp.

On the other hand, sudden violent storms seem to shut elk down. In late September in Idaho we had bulls going all over the place, then a storm blew in and dumped 6 inches of snow. I rejoiced, thinking things would really get wild now, but riding horseback and hiking dozens of miles the next two days, we heard no bulls and saw no fresh tracks in the snow. It seemed like the elk had just vanished. The third day after, clouds broke up and the sun began to melt the snow and it was a pleasant warm time to be out. Suddenly, bulls seemed to be bugling everywhere. On several elk hunts I've witnessed a similar break in action with the onset of violent weather. Perhaps it has something to do with a rapidly falling barometer.

The most predictably poor hunting occurs in hot dry weather when dust builds up on the trails and you end up hunting in a T-shirt. I think it's a misconception that hot weather delays the rut: The period is governed by the timing of calf drop in the spring, not weather in the fall. In any given area, elk must rut at essentially the same time every year to assure a properly timed calving period, so they're breeding, regardless of the weather. But you'll definitely think they're not rutting by the signs of their activities. They'll spend virtually all day in dark, cool timber, and they'll rut and bugle almost exclusively at night.

Even at that you can locate a bull by bugling if you persist. One year my friend Ken Barr and I backpacked for elk in Oregon. For two weeks the sun shined every day. Dust on the trail was six inches deep, and we couldn't tell whether a track had been made yesterday or last week. We got fine suntans, but the hunting was skimpy. We saw virtually no elk, not even cows, where normally we'd seen hundreds. Bugling produced our only action, and in 14 days we bugled in four bulls. We had to persist longer, to dig harder, to put in more miles, to hunt earlier and later than normal, but even under those lousy conditions we found that bulls were bugling.

Whatever the conditions, you can bugle to locate a bull. And that's when the action starts.

Bugle Him In!

Just as there's more than one way to skin the proverbial cat, there's more than one way to hunt a bull elk. Some ways are better than others, however, and I'll stick my neck out and say there's one **best** way to hunt a bull, and that's to bugle him in.

As I've emphasized in Chapter 4, rut hunting allows you to locate bulls by sound and that's a great advantage, but it's not the only one. Equally significant, you can call elk to you. A bull may come to a call for various reasons—to see if the bugler has cows for the taking, to chase off an interloper, to vent his anger by fighting, or just out of curiosity. Probably it makes little difference why they come, but like ducks, turkeys, coyotes and other game, bull elk do come to a call, and that fact makes bugling a deadly form of hunting.

Why is bugling better than stalking? A long time ago someone started the myth that bull elk lose their caution during the rut, so that about all you have to do is to locate one by bugling and then walk up and shoot him. Occasionally bulls do get so frenzied they lose caution, but that's rare. Even during the rut they're sensitive, alert, and very spooky animals, and stalking a bull, particularly close enough for a bow shot, is tough.

To compound the problem of an elk's excellent senses, the bull you're after may be surrounded by a herd of cows and lit-

Normally elk won't come to you over a long distance; you'll have to close the gap, but this bull was an exception. He came to me from a quarter of a mile away until we stared at each other eye-to-eye, 10 yards apart. When I snapped this picture, the elk about broke his neck trying to get away.

tle bulls, so you have to get past the eyes, ears and noses of many animals to collect the bull you want. On top of that, elk tend to hole up in the nastiest vegetation they can find, where silent stalking is impossible. In Idaho my friend Len Garrison hunted with a guide who used his bugle only to locate elk; he then insisted that Len stalk the bulls. Hunting in doghair lodgepole pine, Len and his guide located bugling bulls every day, and Len attempted a number of stalks, but in seven days he never even saw a bull. During that same time my guide and I heard six bulls bugling, and we called three of them within bow range.

The difference is obvious: The stalking hunter moves as his quarry remains stationary, watching and listening, and the dense vegetation of typical elk haunts gives the animals a much greater edge than it gives the hunter. In bugling the roles are reversed. Calling elk to you offers the same advantage that taking a stand offers the deer hunter—you remain still as the game moves to you. That's the greatest edge a hunter, particularly the bowhunter who must get a close shot, can have over any game animal.

CLOSE THE GAP

What does it mean to "bugle in a bull?" When you first locate a bull he may be very close and will come charging at the first toot of your horn, but more often you'll first hear him anywhere from a quarter-mile to a mile away. Rarely will you pull a bull that far. Oregon hunter Billy Cruise tells of bugling from the top of a ridge and having a bull come up from a half-mile below. And one day in Colorado I bugled off a cliff and got a response a quarter-mile below in a basin. I bugled several times, trying to pinpoint the animal's location, and before I knew it the bull was coming my way. Soon he walked into the open 100 yards below and continued steadily up the hill until we stared at each other eye-to-eye, 10 yards apart.

Situations like that are rare. Don't count on calling in a bull from a great distance. At long range, bulls normally just yell back and forth at each other, but they don't come together, so when I say "bugle in a bull" that doesn't mean you sit in one spot and whistle until the elk comes your way, because he probably never will. In most cases, once you've located a bull you'll have to be the aggressor and move in on him, and often you have to get within 100 to 300 yards before he'll come to you.

HURRY UP OR WAIT?

Most hunters I know who've taken several bulls apiece are aggressive; they waste no time in going after a bull. As Larry Jones says, "As far as I'm concerned, there's no tomorrow. As soon as I've got a bull located, I head for him like a bandit."

Ron Granneman figures the faster you can get to a bull after you've first heard him, the better your chances of finding and bugling him in. If a bull is going to bugle a half-dozen times, Granneman reasons, and you wait to make a move until he's bugled three or four times, he may quit bugling and disappear by the time you get close. As long as conditions are right, Granneman thinks you'd better go right after a bull. Fast.

I agree with that, but to qualify it a little I'd emphasize "when conditions are right." Deliberately spooking a bull does you no good, yet that's what you'll do in some situations. If a storm is moving in and the wind is swirling 360 degrees, the chances of your getting within bow range, or even rifle range, of a bull without his smelling you are slim. In Colorado, every morning dawned clear and cold with a stable wind, so conditions were ideal for calling in a bull, but every afternoon about 3 p.m., horrendous thunderstorms developed and the wind began to swirl to create terrible hunting conditions. It was still possible to locate bulls in the afternoon, but with swirling winds you stand little chance of pulling a bull close enough for a shot, so you're better off leaving the elk alone until morning when the wind is stable. Generally a bull will hang out in the same area unless other hunters come along to disturb him.

Jay Elmer has killed several record-class bulls through the cautious approach. He scouts to find a large bull, then he concentrates on killing that one animal. He doesn't hunt on hot afternoons when the bull is brushed up and inactive, and if the wind or surrounding terrain aren't just right for a close-in approach, Jay backs off and waits for better conditions. Jay hasn't killed a lot of elk, but the bulls he has taken are bigger than most hunters will ever see.

LOOK BEFORE YOU LEAP

Let's assume you've heard a bull bugling a half-mile away across a canyon, and because the late-morning breeze is drifting steadily uphill, you've decided to go after him right now. Before you take off, analyze your approach. First, pinpoint the bull. With luck you may see him, so watch a few minutes. Several times I've heard bulls and then, using binoculars, have spotted them moving through the trees.

If you can't see a bull, listen carefully to get a fix on his location. In open, canyon country where sound carries well and travels in a straight line, that may not be difficult, but in convoluted terrain with dense foliage, locating a bull can be tough, so don't take it lightly. On several occasions in northwest Montana, which is extremely dense and broken country, Larry Jones and I would swear up and down we could walk right to a bull only to be fooled.

Early one morning we bugled from a ridgetop, and over a powerful wind we could hear a bull bugling far below. We headed downhill and first ended up in the wrong canyon and couldn't hear the elk at all, so we crossed over a hogback and got in touch. Then our perplexity began in earnest. We knew the bull was still below us, so bugling every few minutes and getting regular answers from the elk, we hiked within 200 yards of the canyon bottom. But then he seemed to be up the far hillside so we climbed up, but then he was below so we charged back down. Vacillating up and down, we spent more than an hour creeping around in confusion, relying on the process of elimination, until we finally found the bull on a small bench 300 yards up the far side of the canyon. Apparently sound echoes and bounces around in that type of enclosed terrain.

THE PROBLEM OF SCENT

Once you've pinpointed a bull, assess the wind carefully. That's the No. 1 consideration in any hunting. A bull may well hear you coming, and he might even see your shadowy form slipping through the trees, and if he doesn't recognize these sounds and sights as human, he may stand firm. But if he once smells you he's gone, so plan to circle around or come in from above or below or whatever you have to do to get the wind in your favor. Generally in early morning and late evening, cooling air drifts downhill so you'll approach from below, but during midday, warming air rises so you'll get above a bull. Prevailing winds, of course, could throw that pattern off completely, so analyze the situation and play the wind to your advantage.

Human scent is such a problem in elk hunting that it deserves more attention than that, and you can take steps to help your cause. The first is to keep clean. We all like to get out and quit taking baths and to smell funky, and that's a great way to break the chains of city life, but it's really not much of an asset in hunting. Loren Butler, who owns a business called Mountain Scent and Bugle Manufacturing, has specialized in studying the nature of scent and its effects on game. Butler points out that scent is cumulative, that is, it builds up on your clothes and skin. In short, the longer you go without washing the worse you stink and the easier a bull elk

Getting dirty in the back country may be fun, but it's not much of an asset in hunting. The cleaner you are the less likely elk are to smell you. Human scent is the No. 1 consideration as you move in on a bull.

will smell you. If you've bathed and washed your clothes, an elk might smell you at 50 yards; if you're packing a week's worth of BO, he conceivably could smell you at 500 yards.

Butler suggests washing with baking soda and putting your clothes in a bag with baking soda. Soda neutralizes bacteria that create human odor, and it absorbs odor. If you're clean, a commercial coverup scent, such as pine or cedar extract, will help mask your odor, although masking scents aren't magic and probably won't help much if you aren't reasonably clean. As Butler said, "Nothing will mask a 24-hour accumulation of human odor."

MOVING IN

If a bull is some distance away, move fast to close the gap. If he's across a canyon, that could take an hour or more, and the elk could do a lot of moving in that time, so bugle every 10 minutes or so to keep tabs on him and to keep him hot. Most bulls will answer when you bugle, and that tells you what they're doing.

Close in steadily until you're within 300 to 400 yards, then slow down and move cautiously. That's not necessarily to be more quiet, because elk themselves are noisy. An approaching bull can sound like Godzilla crunching through the brush, so some "approaching bull" noise on your part isn't a disaster. The problem is that a bull often is closer than he sounds and if you move too fast, you inadvertently could walk right into him. As a general rule, the closer you get, the better your chances for bugling him in so you want to get close, but unless you know exactly where he is—and you rarely will—don't push your luck. Start conservatively, and once you get within 100 to 200 yards, stop and prepare to bugle the bull to you. If he won't come that far, you can always move in later.

Keeping the wind in your favor is so critical that it's worth mentioning again here. Before the hunt, tie a light thread or a string with a duck feather on your bow to indicate wind direction; or you can sift dust through your hands, light a match to watch the smoke, or notice the movements of hanging moss to monitor the slightest breeze. If you find the wind has shifted on you, move fast to get it right. It's better to run a half-circle around a bull, crashing like a charging buffalo, than it is to let the bull smell you.

BUGLE WITH CARE

Once you're within a bull's territory, never bugle carelessly. Assume you'll call in a bull every time you blow a call and you'll never get caught off guard, or with your pants down, as they say. Every hunter has a repertoire of "call of nature" stories, and one of my favorites well illustrates this point.

Ken Barr, a hunting friend from Oregon, and I had heard a bull right at daybreak. The animal was a long way off, more than a half-mile we figured, so we hiked up the mountain toward him. We'd covered about half the distance when Ken had to answer nature's call.

"I'll walk on ahead and give a toot," I said. "Just to see where he's at."

At the edge of a meadow I paused in the timber and whistled high and loud on my elk call. The bull responded immediately with a hoarse bellow.

"Ken," I whispered. "He's not as far as we thought."

Just then the bull bugled again. Much closer.

Ken! You'd better hurry up. He's coming."

Ken had heard all of this and didn't need me to tell him the story. He came running up the hill, holding up his pants with one hand, carrying his bow and pack in the other.

We dived into a clump of spruce trees and had barely gotten out of sight when the bull charged into view at the top of the meadow, 100 yards away. He stopped, bugled, and then thundered down towards us. At 50 yards, he slid to a halt, thrashed a small tree with his antlers, braying and squealing like a donkey, and then ran straight at us. At 20 yards I drew my bow and as the bull trotted by, close enough to spit on, I launched an arrow a foot over his back. The bull ran on by into the timber below and stopped at 40 yards. I nocked a second arrow, but shaken now, I didn't notice that a limb had hooked inside the lower limb of my bow, and when I released, the arrow flipped sideways and plowed into the ground halfway between me and the bull. He'd had enough of that nonsense and disappeared. That bull was as hot as any I've bugled in and he should have been dead, but I'd bugled carelessly and got caught off guard. The point should be clear: Before you bugle, be prepared!

THE SETUP

A setup has two components: Shooting lanes and a blind. My descriptions here of a good setup applies primarily to bowhunting because an archer must work a bull in very close, but the same principles apply to rifle hunting. The more meticulous any hunter is about setting up, the better are his chances for a clean shot.

It does little good to bugle in a bull if you can't shoot him, so first look for a spot with open shooting lanes. In country with sparse vegetation that may be no real problem. For example, in Colorado two friends and I had clear shots at every elk that approached within 50 yards, but in other regions it hasn't been that easy.

Our first evening in Montana, Larry Jones bugled a large bull within six yards. Larry worked on the bull for more than an hour, but in the bull's alder-jungle hangout, Larry was unable to get a clear shot, so he backed off and left the bull undisturbed.

The next morning we returned and the animal was still there, bugling like crazy. We stalked within 100 yards and began to hurl insults at him. That made him good and mad and soon he was rolling toward us making noise like a Vietnam jungle crusher. He loomed into view at 25 yards and stopped at 15 to bugle, then he started working on a tree, shredding the bark into long strips with his brow tines and chewing the strips. I stared into his bloodshot eyes and could hear his raspy breathing and low grunting as Larry bugled behind me, trying to pull the bull into the open. The bull was so close, 10 to 15 yards, I couldn't move, but even at that there was no way I could thread an arrow through the tangled limbs between me and the bull. I waited. Finally, tired of playing games, the animal walked away. For the second time in 24 hours that elk had been closer than 15 yards to hunters and had escaped unscathed.

Experiences like that make you consider bowling as a hobby. And they make you think deeply about your setup. Always look for a spot—a meadow, clearing, a grove of open timber—where an approaching bull must come into the open, and remember that bulls often will circle to get your wind. So look for a spot not only with shooting lanes out front, on the upwind side where you **hope** a bull will come in; but on the

Once you get within a bull's territory, never bugle carelessly. Assume an elk will come on the run every time you blow your call, and prepare accordingly. Here Larry Jones is bugling to locate a bull. Notice how his total camouflage helps conceal him among these willow trees.

If you can find three or four trees in a circle, get in the midst of them and break out branches to form shooting lanes in all directions, then hold your bow or rifle up, ready to shoot, as I'm doing here. When a bull approaches you simply draw and release. An incoming bull won't spot you if you're totally concealed like this.

downwind side, too, where the bull **probably** will come in.

THE BLIND

A good blind has to conceal you and provide plenty of room for shooting. It starts with camouflage. I know hunters who spurn face paint and other camouflage, and many of them have killed more than their share of elk. I think in the long run, however, that good camouflage pays, not only because it helps you to hide but because it gives you confidence in tight situations, and that confidence makes you a better hunter. I wear a camouflage hat, face paint, green gloves, pants and shirt, and paint my bow flat black and green. That's the first part of effective blinding.

The second part is cover, and perhaps the ideal cover is a cluster of trees. If you can find three or four trees in a circle, get in the midst of them and break branches out of the way to clear shooting holes in all directions. Don't worry about snapping branches because it just sounds like a bull raking a tree with his antlers. In this position you're surrounded by foliage, and as long as you stay still, no incoming bull will see you.

To shoot, stand with your bow or rifle in a ready position. Holding up a bow can tire your arm, so before the hunt sew a pocket on your hunting pants to rest the lower tip of your bow in, which supports the bow at shooting level. When an elk comes within range, you simply draw and shoot with very little movement.

Larry Jones raises an interesting point about blinding cover. As he points out, when a bull comes to your call he expects to see another bull there. If he doesn't, and there's no cover large enough to conceal an elk, he'll get suspicious in a hurry, so Larry suggests blinding in cover that could hide a bull.

Of course, perfect stand sites aren't scattered everywhere you want them. If you can't find good trees for blinding, stand or kneel with a bush, the trunk of a big tree, or a rock behind you so you're not silhouetted. If you're well camouflaged, an open blind like this can be effective, and it's preferable over cover that's too heavy.

Gary Alt and I learned that the hard way. We were working on a bull in open lodgepole pine where it seemed that getting a clear shot would be a cinch. When the bull started our way, Gary hurriedly knelt behind a gnarled little pine and I lay behind a tree uphill. When I bugled, a 5-point bull with a silvery, almost-white coat sauntered into view 80 yards below and marched toward us. At 30 yards Gary drew his bow and waited as the bull came closer and closer. The animal finally stopped just opposite Gary's blind tree, broadside, and I expected a flurry of action. But Gary remained frozen, his bow at full draw, and finally the bull got suspicious and bolted.

"Why didn't you shoot?" I asked, incredulous.

"Look at this," Gary said, pointing to the gnarled pine. "His chest was right behind those branches, and there's no way I could slip an arrow through here. If he'd taken one more step I'd have had him."

So near yet so far, and it was our own fault. If we'd taken time to set up right and clear shooting holes, Gary would have killed that bull. We paced off the distance from Gary's knee prints in the sand to the bull's tracks. Ten feet.

TO BUGLE OR NOT TO BUGLE

As discussed in Chapter 3, one secret to bugling in a bull is variety. You bugle, bray, grunt and rake a tree in various combinations to find the mix that enrages a bull. Then you know you're on the right track.

But varied sounds aren't the whole secret: Timing is important, too. The amount of your bugling is a hotly debated subject. Some hunters say bugling should be kept to a minimum. They believe you should let the bull be the aggressor and that you should bugle only in response to his calling. In other words, you let him set the tempo of the conflict.

Here's the reasoning. First, if you bugle too much, a bull may recognize you as a phony and get suspicious. Indeed, if you're blowing a phony-sounding whistle, that's a distinct possibility, but if you've perfected your bugling, that argument doesn't hold up. I've bugled repeatedly at bulls within 5-20 yards and have never seen one spook as a result. A bull walked within 20 yards of Rich LaRocco and me and I shrilled time after time on a reed-type call, and the bull never even glanced in my direction. The more I blew the more intent he got on destroying a Christmas tree, and he'd have done a good job if Rich hadn't thumped him with an arrow.

Another argument against bugling too much is that you'll intimidate a bull and run him off. I suppose that could happen, but normally your bugling simply triggers a bugling response from the bull and incites him to greater anger. Certainly, if a bull is hot and is coming right in, there's little need to bugle a lot or even at all; one squeal and a little tree raking might bring him on the run, so hold it to that. Don't do anything more than is necessary to pull the bull in.

But normally you'll have to do much more. A calm bull is a cautious bull, and cautious bulls are hard to fool. Larry Jones consistently calls in bulls close enough to hit with a pea shooter, and his objective in bugling is to excite a bull, to stir him up so he'll make mistakes. If you bugle only occasionally, say every five to ten minutes, most bulls will just bugle back and you'll have a fine hollering match. Some hunters call that "social bugling." Larry doesn't let that happen. He figures if a bull gets bored with a situation and starts drifting off, pulling him back will be harder than ever, so Larry starts right in, as soon as he's set up, bugling frequently and grunting and raking on a tree. He's the aggressor, the one who sets the tempo. He doesn't wait for the bull to bugle so he can answer; he bugles first to make that bull answer him.

Mike Schlegel, a well-known Idaho hunter, takes a similar approach. When he gets in close to a bull, he bugles at least as often and sometimes twice as often as the bull, and between bugles he grunts and beats on a tree.

QUIET TIME

That doesn't mean you constantly make a racket in any situation. Even the hottest bull pauses during his thrashing and bugling to sniff the air and look around, so your bugling and raking should contain similar natural pauses. A very general rule might be to bugle every three to five minutes, raking and grunting in between, but that could vary greatly from one situation to another. In dealing with a hot bull you might bugle once a minute or more often. From experience you'll learn intuitively how much to bugle and when to be quiet.

Quiet periods not only create realism, but they're critical for monitoring a bull's progress, too. If an elk catches you in the middle of a bugle or banging on a tree, he'll pinpoint you

A bowhunter rarely has to shoot farther than 30 to 40 yards. Larry Jones (right) bugled this bull in and Andy Day shot it at a range of 12 feet. This bull scores 312. (Photo courtesy Larry D. Jones)

instantly and that brings down the curtain on your act. You'll have no problem following the approach of some bulls as they smash trees and roar louder and louder, but other animals will come in cautiously, perhaps not bugling at all. You may hear nothing but the crack of a twig or heavy breathing, and you'll feel like a goat staked out for leopard bait, wondering when something's going to pounce on you. In any setup, take plenty of time to watch and listen carefully to keep from getting caught off guard.

There are exceptions to every rule, but normally, just before a bull comes into view, usually 50 to 75 yards out, you'll want to shut up completely. Just stand silent and motionless, ready to shoot. Don't worry about the bull's finding you. He knows right where you are.

GETTING THE SHOT

Some hunters say that as long as a bull is coming your way, let him come. Certainly a bowhunter wants to get the surest shot possible, but I think you can carry that too far. It's not unusual to pull an elk within five to ten yards or less—the closest I've seen was the bull that stood ten feet from Gary Alt—which seems ideal, but at that range a bull can sense your slightest odor or movement, and he's liable to explode in a blur of motion before you can shoot. Farther out he might not be so wire tight, so in my opinion a 30-yard shot at a calm bull is better than a 5-yard shot at one that's tensed, ready to bolt. Picking the right time to shoot is a matter of judgment, but a bowhunter rarely has reason to shoot farther than 30 to 40 yards. Within that range I'd say take the first clean chest shot—from the side into the heart and lungs—you can get. That's the only place to shoot an elk with an arrow. Of course, this matter of shooting distance and shot placement isn't as critical with firearms hunters. Hunting with a rifle, you might reasonably take a neck shot at 100 yards.

Occasionally an animal will hang up just out of range, probably because he's suspicious about not finding the bull he expected to see. If that happens try a ventriloquist's act by turning slowly and bugling away from the bull. Sometimes that's just enough to pull him on in. The mouth diaphragm or voice bugling are ideal during this critical, close-in period because you can chirp or grunt without moving your hands to lift a call.

THE WAY IT SHOULD BE

Here's a "typical" bugling sequence that took place in northwest Colorado in the sagebrush-and-aspen country west of Meeker. Early in the morning a bull bugled at the bottom of a canyon, and I went down after him. Through repeated bugling back and forth I followed him by sound up the far side of the canyon through an aspen park. I felt sure he'd stopped to bed in a Douglas fir grove on top of a knoll, so approaching that spot I hid behind a head-high fir tree.

With my knife, I sliced several branches halfway through and beat them out of the way with a stick to clear shooting holes. I continued to rake the tree for 10 seconds to sound like a mad bull, then I blew a shrill challenge on my bugle. Just up the hill a bull brayed a couple of times. In response to that I bugled sharply and banged on the tree some more.

Seconds later a bull walked into the open, 50 yards away.

At 30 yards he stopped and grunted, his neck heaving like a bellows. With him that close I couldn't bugle or even blink an eye, so I just held my bow up and waited. The elk turned and started to walk uphill and I drew my bow. The bull noticed the movement and stopped to glower at me. Just as he paused my arrow caught him behind the front shoulder. He ran 200 yards and piled up.

That's bugling in a bull.

Here's the bull I killed after a "typical" bugling sequence near Meeker, Colorado. After a 30-yard shot he ran only 200 yards before he piled up. That's the way bugling in a bull should work.

More on Bugling

That pretty well sums up the mechanics of calling in a bull. All bugling is a variation on that basic theme, but there's one catch—it doesn't always work that smoothly. Just when you think you've got elk hunting figured out and you're feeling pretty smart, a crafty bull comes along to make you look like a fool.

That doesn't mean bugling doesn't work, just that you've still got something to learn. I suspect thathunterswho underrate the value of bugling have tried calling in a bull once or twice, and because an addlebrained animal didn't brazenly walk into the open begging to get shot, they've assumed it doesn't really work. Make no mistake—on occasion you'll bugle in a bull so easily you'll feel guilty about shooting him, but don't let that get you down. Not every bull will come on the run, and if you spend enough time in the woods chasing elk, you'll pay your dues.   I honestly think you can bugle in most bulls you hear, but don't expect miracles. Getting some bulls in takes relentless persistence and an instinct for making the right moves at the right time. I've hesitated to lay down any rules about bugling because exceptions may outnumber the rules, but you have to start some place, so that's what I've done in Chapter 5. Now I'll explore some of the exceptions and how to deal with them.

Over the long I think you'll do best by hunting alone. If you've got a good setup and are patient, you can wait out a bull and he'll eventually present a broadside shot. This little 5-point started straight for me, but then he swung wide and presented a broadside, 30-yard shot.

THE BUDDY SYSTEM

Over the long haul I think a lone hunter is more efficient than two or more hunters together. A single hunter can move quickly to get into position, and he has no communication problems; the left hand doesn't have to worry about what the right hand is doing.

It is true that hunting alone has its drawbacks. When you bugle in a bull, he's coming to the call, so he might walk straight at you and a head-on shot is poor, particularly for a bowhunter. But if you've got a good setup and are patient, you can wait out a bull and he'll eventually present a broadside shot. Most really successful hunters generally hunt alone. Ron Granneman has killed 14 bulls in 14 years of hunting, and he's been alone on every kill. Jay Elmer killed world-record bulls two consecutive years, and he was by himself each time.

On the other hand, the buddy system has its strong points.

The idea of bugling with a partner is to have a shooter out front with the bugler hidden behind, so that on his way to the bugle, the bull walks unsuspectingly past the shooter to present an easy shot.

The method works, but it's not foolproof. Remember that the bull is coming to the call, so he may circle out of range of the shooter. Here's an example. Gary Alt and I moved in on a bull. Gary set up on the downhill side between me and the bull, and I bugled from behind. The elk didn't bugle at all, but we could hear him breaking limbs as he came our way. The setup looked perfect at first, but then something went wrong. Instead of coming straight in, the bull circled wide of Gary, probably to get our wind, and came directly to me. Gary couldn't get a shot, and since I'd already filled my tag, I could do nothing but smile at the five-point bull standing broadside at 25 yards. To prevent that, the shooter and bugler should stay reasonably close together, say within 30 to 50 yards.

THE MISSED SHOT

Every bowhunter has heard this: "How could you miss something as big as an elk at 10 yards?"

Comments like that do little to lift your spirits just after you've blown the chance of a lifetime, but if you do miss a shot, take heart. If you play your cards—or bugle—right, you could get a second chance. Or third. Or fourth. At least that's the case if you're bowhunting. A bull coming to your call expects to find another elk, so he's not really tensed up. When your bow thunks lightly and an arrow hisses past his back, the elk probably will jump and run, but only because he's startled. Unless he's smelled or seen you he still doesn't know a human being is present. If you give a shrill blast on your call as soon as the bull bolts, you often can bring him right back in.

In Montana I stumbled into a herd of elk and they took off running. I jumped behind a stump and blasted on my bugle and the elk stopped. Over the next five minutes I bugled several times and beat on a tree with a club. Pretty soon a bull began to rake a tree and grunt and squeal. In response I played like an outraged bull and bugled shrilly and thrashed some branches. Apparently that convinced the bull I was a bull for real because he started my way, his antlers visible over the brush. The breeze was drifting downhill, so the bull started to angle below me to get my scent. The best shooting lane was straight downhill but I couldn't wait until he got there or he'd smell me, so as he approached an opening to the right I drew and shot. The bull was only 20 yards away, but the arrow nicked a branch and bounced up and hit another branch and smacked into the ground short of the elk. He whirled and ran. Before he'd covered 50 yards I roared on my bugle. The bull stopped short. He looked back over his shoulder. Then he turned and ambled right back to me, this time 30 yards out. At full draw I followed until his chest was in the clear, being careful not to hit those limbs again, but my perfectly placed arrow caught a different branch and glanced away at a 45-degree angle. I tried bugling the elk into range a third time, but he'd have none of that.

I've seen missed bulls bugled in as many as four times. That may not say much for somebody's shooting ability, but don't ignore this important point—you can pull a bull back for a second try if you get right on the horn.

HOW LONG SHOULD YOU BUGLE?

Hunters frequently ask, "How long does it take to bugle in a bull?" On that bull near Meeker, Colorado, mentioned at the end of Chapter 5, less than five minutes elapsed from the time I set up until the shot. Ken Barr and I almost got run over by the "call of nature" bull no more than 10 minutes after the first time we'd heard him. Obviously bugling in a bull may not take long at all.

But those are unusual cases. Most elk are cautious. Often a bull may spend more than an hour covering 50 yards as he smashes trees, bugles, sniffs the air and generally works himself into a lather. Rutting bulls aren't necessarily out of their minds, and most will approach slowly. Just for the sake of discussion I'll say the average bugling time, after you first set up, is an hour, but it could take three to four hours to draw an elk into shooting range, so don't get in a hurry. Patience may be the real secret behind successful elk hunting. If you're in a hurry to see something happen, you'll forever be frustrated.

My friend Larry Jones regularly calls bulls within bow

Ron Granneman is one hunter who believes in hunting alone. Granneman has killed 14 bulls in 14 years, and he's taken every one while hunting by himself. Out of those 14 bulls, 8 qualify for the Pope and Young record book. This bull scores 336.

range not just because he's a good caller but because he's undaunted in persistence. One day Larry first heard a bull bugling at 7 a.m. He moved in close and got the bull heated up, and a couple of times Larry could see the animal's legs only yards away, but the timber was so dense he couldn't get a shot and eventually the bull drifted away.

Larry continued to search and to bugle. For more than an hour he never heard nor saw the elk, but sensing the bull was still in the area, he stayed alert and careful. He found the elk's tracks and followed them for some distance. When they led to a thick stand of yew trees, Larry figured the bull might hide there, so he blinded in and began to bugle. After several minutes the furtive bull returned the challenge, and Larry finally coaxed him into the open, and killed him with a lung shot at 20 yards. The time was 11 a.m., four hours after the start of the encounter.

STICK AND MOVE

As I've said, a good starting distance for a setup is 100 to

On the other hand, the buddy system can be effective, too. Bowhunters must be careful not to set up too far apart, but that's not as critical in rifle hunting.

300 yards, but sometimes that's not close enough. If you set up and start bugling, and nothing seems to happen, you might have to pressure the bull to get something going. If you've bugled for 15 to 20 minutes and the bull just hollers back but doesn't move, or if he seems to be losing interest and drifting away, try moving in. Generally, the closer you get without spooking him—and indeed you do have to be careful any time you move—the more likely you are to bugle him in.

Rich LaRocco and I used stick-and-move tactics to kill a bull in Colorado. We'd been traveling the side of a canyon all morning, bugling regularly, trying to locate a bull when we finally heard one far across the canyon at 1 p.m. We took our time getting to him, working around to get the wind just right, procrastinating to make the grand assault in the cool of the evening when the bull would be more active. At 5 p.m. we set up within 200 to 300 yards of the bull and started bugling. The bull whistled back regularly, but after 20 minutes he'd come no closer, so we left our blinds and moved 100 yards toward him. Again we set up and bugled, and again he called back, but after 10 minutes, his bugling became fainter. Apparently he was wandering away.

Again, we hurried forward and set up, and at that point we bugled for 20 minutes and got no reply at all. The woods were silent except for the groan of wind from a rising thunderstorm. Possibly we'd spooked him and should have given up. But, no, we felt sure he was just playing cat and mouse, so we kept the pressure on.

We advanced another 100 yards until we came to a small meadow. There Rich knelt behind a chest-high fir tree at the edge of a meadow, and I lay on a bank about 20 yards to the side. The instant I bugled the bull screamed back and swaggered into view at the far edge of the meadow, not 70 yards away. As the elk walked toward us I bugled again and beat on a tree to hold his attention. He stopped 20 yards from Rich and went to work on a Christmas tree, and just then, right after 6 p.m., Rich hit him behind the front shoulder with an arrow. We found the fine 5-point a half-hour later in the middle of a meadow. We spent half the night in a driving thundershower skinning the elk.

THE SILENT BULL

Anytime you move on an elk, be cautious; he could be playing tricks. Anybody who's done much elk hunting has encountered the silent bull, and Gary Alt had that pleasure on his very first elk hunt. From the far side of a canyon Gary spotted a bull on a hillside, so he hiked close to the bull, set up and started bugling. He called patiently for 20 minutes but during that time he got absolutely no response. He decided the bull wasn't interested and stepped out from his hiding place, and at that moment he noticed antlers just opposite the clump of trees he'd been hiding behind. The bull had walked

Rich LaRocco shot this bull at 20 yards after we'd set up four different times. We spent half the night in a driving thunderstorm gutting and skinning this bull.

within seven paces of Gary and had never let out a peep.

On that same trip Gary and I bugled in several other bulls that came in regularly but without bugling. It was early in the rut, about the first of September, and they seemed to come in more out of curiosity than the desire to fight.

Also, a bull could be red-hot but may not bugle much. In Idaho Len Garrison and I bugled near the top of a long draw and heard a bull down the hill. We moved down to set up and I bugled vociferously. The bull answered a couple of times but never with much enthusiasm. Twice we moved closer and at one point we heard his antlers clattering on a tree, so we knew he wasn't far away. But as near as we could tell the bull wasn't getting steamed up, and he quit bugling altogether after that.

"Maybe we're not pushing him hard enough," I whispered to Len. "Let's get right in his hip pocket and make him bugle."

We started to make one last move when we spotted the antlers, no more than 20 yards away. The bull had been coming right to us, and we'd met him head on. He saw us at the same instant and thundered away.

Looking where he'd been, we discovered he'd torn up a patch of timber 100 feet square. It looked like someone had been in there with a bulldozer. Our bugling had got him raging mad, and he'd taken out his wrath on the local shrubbery, but he had hardly bugled at all. Don't be hasty in making judgments. Listen and watch carefully before you make any fast moves.

THE RUNNING BULL

It's not unusual to have a bull run away from you. It could be because he's smelled you, but if that's the case he'll probably just quit bugling and disappear, and that's the end of that hunt.

But what about the bull that runs away but keeps right on bugling? You might think you've blown it with your calling, but chances are you didn't. Most likely that's a herd bull that thinks you're another elk, and he's trying to keep his cows away from you. A harem master's big concern is to horde his cows, and most seem to prefer running away with their harems than fighting over them. As long as you stay some distance away, a herd bull will bugle at you continually, but as soon as you get close enough to seem threatening, he'll pack up his cows and hightail it.

You can bugle in a herd bull, but it often takes time and physical endurance. Most experienced buglers I know will pursue a running bull, trying to stay within a quarter-mile or so, bugling and pushing the bull until he gets irritated enough to stop and battle.

Mike Schlegel tells of one herd bull he antagonized that way. Schlegel began working on the animal early in the morning and the bull bugled steadily, but every time Mike got within 200 yards or so the bull took off running. Mike tried to keep up, which was no easy task in the steep jungles of northern Idaho, and several times he got close, but each time he started bugling the bull ran off. Finally Mike shut up altogether and sneaked quietly within 50 yards of the bull, got set up, and cut loose with some defiant bugling and grunting. The 6-point bull, angered by this sneaky upstart, charged down the hill and Mike nailed him at 10 yards.

Herd bulls often bugle continually, so you can follow their progress fairly easily. If you're fast enough, you can run ahead of the herd and waylay them. Elk do move out, however, so you'd better be in some fine shape before you try that.

Dealing with herd bulls is a case where two hunters can work well together. One stays at a distance, blowing his call to keep the bull angry and bugling, and the other runs ahead to intercept the bull, or he sneaks in for a shot.

Outfitter Ed McCallum and I made that work in Idaho. About noon we heard an unbelievable explosion of squealing and bugling a half-mile away. With all that racket we felt sure a herd bull was involved (it turned out there were three bulls there). On previous days we'd had problems with herd bulls running from us so rather than trying to bugle this one in, we decided to try a different approach. Ed would stay 300 yards away to bugle, and I would stalk in silently.

I took off toward the elk, and every time Ed whistled, the bulls cut loose with a cacophony of braying and squealing. It sounded like two Hereford bulls with their tails tied together. They were so preoccupied with carrying on that I had no trouble sneaking within 50 yards. In more open country I'd have kept quiet and stalked in for a shot, but here the bulls were

Outfitter Ed McCallum and I had had trouble with herd bulls running from us so we teamed up to fool this animal. Ed stayed about 300 yards away as I stalked within 50 yards. At that range I bugled and the bull walked right to me.

ensconced in a jungle where sneaking within range seemed impossible. But this close I figured one might impulsively come on the run, so I blew a shriek on my call. A fine 6-point emerged and met his waterloo at 30 yards.

THE SCREAMER BULL

One morning Ed McCallum and I were wandering through the dense lodgepole pine, trying to locate a bull. From a ridge we bugled several times, but we got no answer and moved on. We'd walked no more than 200 yards when, seemingly right beside us, a bull cut loose with a terrible scream that definitely was not meant as a friendly greeting. The sudden, deafening sound sent shivers down our spines. Regaining our composure, we bugled and searched, but we never saw nor heard that bull again.

Later that day in a different area, the same thing happened. A bull screamed one time, seemingly right next to us. Again we came unglued.

"That son of a gun," I said to Ed. "I'm getting tired of having those turkeys scream and hide. Watch this!"

I grabbed a big stick and went nuts, pounding on trees and bugling, frantic to get that screamer bull to come out and fight like a man. We never heard another sound, but late that evening we spotted a big bull with cows not far from where we'd gotten screamed at. We felt sure this bull was the culprit.

Both of those screamer bulls had to have heard our bugling, and they probably had heard us walking through the woods. They undoubtedly thought we were eager bulls invading their territory. I think those raucous screams were warning threats that meant, "Stay away! These cows are mine!"

I've talked to other hunters who've had similar experiences, and they've had no better luck at dealing with those rude beasts than I have. That's an exception to the idea that you can bugle in any bull you hear.

Or maybe those aren't bulls after all. Would you believe Sasquatch?

THE ALLIGATOR BULL

Some hunters in Montana told me about alligator bulls, which was a new one on me. I didn't know what that meant. Hunting a few days later I heard a bull across a canyon, but when I got close he wouldn't bugle. Fresh sign told me he was close by, so I hid and taunted him with my bugle. No answer. Then in the deep, awesome silence of brooding timber a twig snapped. That was the only sound, but make no mistake, it was made by an animal, and that animal was sneaking up on me. More silence. Then as intangibly as fog rising from the ground the massive rack of a 6-point bull appeared over a clump of Christmas trees 10 yards above me. Then the eyes appeared. That's all. The eyes and the top of the head. Just like an alligator lying in the water. So that's what they meant. The skulking brute stared with bulging, bloodshot eyes for a half-minute, and then he vanished as silently as he'd appeared.

Alligator bulls. I don't know what to do with those either. Maybe bulldog them and tie a rope around their jaws.

Other Approaches to Hunting

Bugling in a bull isn't the only way to hunt early-season elk. In fact, some hunters would say it's not even the best way, and for them it might not be. There are alternatives to straight bugling that might suit your hunting territory or your personality better.

AMBUSH

Elk generally follow fairly set routines, but in some regions these are hard to discern. In others they're more distinct. In Arizona, for example, water, feed and bedding sites may be far apart, and the hunter who knows the location of these areas and travel routes between stands a good chance of ambushing a bull. Mike Cupell, who has killed a number of bulls in Arizona, has intimate knowledge of his area and often can predict where elk are going. He gets out before daylight to locate an animal by bugling, then often, rather than approaching the bull directly, he anticipates where the elk will go and moves ahead to ambush the animal.

One day Mike and well-known bowhunter Doug Kittredge heard bugling and spotted a bull with cows. Already the animals were drifting toward their bedding area. Mike knew that keeping up with them would be tough, so he suggested

Mike Cupell uses his knowledge of elk movements in Arizona to ambush animals as they travel from feeding to bedding areas. Obviously Cupell believes in camouflage.

that he and Doug circle wide, running as fast as possible, to come in on the back side of a low ridge one and a half miles away. From scouting Mike knew that's where the elk would bed for the day. The hunters beat the elk there, and as bugling from the approaching herd grew closer, the hunters maneuvered to get in the path of the elk. One bull bedded very near them and they missed that one, but shortly after, Mike blew his call and a big bull rushed in from nearby and Kittredge nailed him. The bull scored 380-2/8, at that time large enough to qualify as the Pope and Young world record.

STALKING

In that case, Mike Cupell combined ambush techniques with bugling. Jay Elmer, another Arizona bowhunter, uses his knowledge of the country to ambush animals, but he doesn't bugle at all. Rather he stalks because he thinks that's the surest way to kill a big bull.

Jay is a trophy hunter. Through scouting he locates one big bull that he wants, and he concentrates strictly on killing that one animal. He reasons that if he bugles and gets the bull coming in, and conditions turn sour—say the wind shifts or the bull circles out of range and smells him—he's had it. That may be the last chance he'll get at that bull. In contrast, Jay thinks he can make any number of stalks without spooking a bull. First, he hunts only early and late when the bull is moving on his own and is most visible; he stays away during midday when the animal is bedded. Then as he stalks he monitors conditions continuously. If the wind isn't just right, other elk get in his way, or something else is wrong, he backs off and tries to approach from a different angle or waits for a better all-around situation.

He combines this careful-stalking philosophy with his knowledge of the country to ambush a bull in his daily movements. Early one morning he heard a bull bugling and he knew the bull and his cows were moving, so Jay placed himself in their path as they left water and headed toward a bedding ridge. He followed the herd's progress by the bugling of the bull. Several times Jay stalked in front of the elk as they meandered along, but each time something seemed wrong and he backed off. Finally about 8:30 he came to a shallow draw where he'd previously seen a well-used elk

Jay Elmer uses ambush and stalking techniques to pursue trophy bulls. Elmer tried several stalks before he committed himself and moved in for the shot on this bull. The score of this animal is 389 2/8, and it was the Pope and Young world record. It has since been superseded by a larger elk killed in Montana. (Photo courtesy Jay Elmer)

trail. He took a stand at the edge of the draw, expecting the elk to follow the same trail they'd used before. They did and Jay shot the bull at 20 yards. It scored 389-2/8, large enough to eclipse Doug Kittredge's bull as the world record.

STILL HUNTING

In stalking you sneak up on an animal you've already seen or heard. In contrast, still hunting means you slip quietly through the woods, trying to spot animals at close range before they see you. In some cases still hunting can be an excellent way to hunt elk.

Shari Fraker is primarily a still hunter. She laughs that she started out sneaking through the woods because she didn't know that wasn't the way to hunt elk. Fortunately for her, her wrong approach has been so successful that she's continually called upon to give elk-hunting seminars.

One reason she sticks with sneak hunting, opposed to bugl-

Shari Fraker is primarily a still hunter. She sneaks through the woods quietly for hours on end. She shuns bugling because she doesn't want elk to know she's anywhere around. (Photo courtesy Shari Fraker)

ing, is that so many other hunters are bugling in her area these days that she thinks bulls are getting call shy. She feels more confident if elk don't know she's anywhere around.

The most important step in sneak hunting, Fraker says, is knowing where to sneak. Setting out blindly, you could creep around for days without running into elk. Fraker scouts intensively to eliminate that possibility. When she starts hunting she knows for sure that she's close to elk, and she has a definite hunting plan in mind. The first day she follows Plan A. If that doesn't work, she goes to Plan B and so forth.

"I'm very slow," Fraker said. "Perhaps a lot of men won't hunt the way I do because they're bigger and have to bend over and work harder at slipping silently through the woods.

I hunt all day, just taking my time and watching and listening and smelling until I locate elk."

Her object is to remain undetected, so she wears flexible tennis shoes that allow her to tiptoe, and she wears complete camouflage, including face paint. Rather than traditional green clothing, however, she favors brown so that if animals do spot her, they might mistake her for another elk. Of course, she always hunts into the wind, but knowing an errant breeze could give her away, she frequently stomps in fresh elk manure to help mask her scent.

Still hunting is especially apropos if bulls aren't bugling and you're not picky about the kind of elk you shoot. You'll do best when animals are active. It's possible to slip up on bedded elk—I did it twice in one day—but it's not likely. In sunny weather elk probably will be moving only the first and last hours of daylight, but on overcast days, they might feed throughout the day.

In any elk hunting use all of your senses. As I've stressed, you'll often smell elk before you see them, and you'll hear them, too. One drizzly afternoon I was still hunting and heard clomp, clomp, clomp. Silence. Clomp, clomp. It had to be the sound of hooves. For five minutes I listened and crept ahead, trying to zero in on the sound. Suddenly a cow elk appeared and began chomping on an alder tree. I brought her down with an arrow at 30 yards.

On another overcast afternoon I heard a slight rustling. It could have been a chickaree or a grouse. Swish, swish. But it was too steady for small creatures. After a few minutes of that, six elk fed into view. I'd been hearing their legs brushing through huckleberry bushes. I killed a cow from that herd.

STAND HUNTING

It's no secret that stand hunting is a deadly art. The hunter stays motionless and quiet as animals walk to him, and no situation could be more ideal, especially for bowhunters.

The real challenge in stand hunting is knowing where to put the stand. In Arizona and other parts of the Southwest, where water is very limited, elk rely heavily on stock tanks for water, and many elk are killed by hunters on stands overlooking waterholes. Arizona hunters tell me competition

I killed this cow elk while still hunting on a dark drizzly afternoon. I heard the animal clomping my way long before she ever came into view.

for good waterholes has gotten pretty stiff. Mike Cupell said that he's found that many animals, and often the biggest ones, avoid large stock tanks and drink at small seeps and trickles of water, so these covert water sources might be more productive than the obvious ones. It should go without saying that waterhole hunting is most deadly during dry weather.

Cupell also said that elk walk fences for great distances, so fencelines are potentially good spots for stands. I can't verify that because I've never hunted country with fences. Before putting a stand anywhere, of course, you evaluate the situation in terms of fresh sign.

A good place to take a stand is near a fresh wallow. Murky water and fresh tracks tell you that a bull has used this wallow recently, so this might be a good site for a tree stand.

John Lamicq, a well-known outfitter and guide in Colorado, uses tree stands regularly in his operation. He said that in 1982, his hunters got 11 close shots at elk, and one hunter in a tree stand overlooking a wallow killed a 7x7 bull.

Any fresh wallow—with emphasis on fresh—is a good place for a stand. Rutting bulls will return to the same wallow time after time to roll and coat themselves with mud. Lamicq said he's found wallow stands consistently effective only in hot, dry weather; when weather turns cold and damp, bulls don't use them regularly enough to warrant putting stands there.

In traveling from feeding to bedding areas, especially in heavy timber where movements are restricted, elk form trails as distinct as cattle trails. Lamicq often places stands overlooking these trails as long as he finds fresh tracks there.

Any slight human disturbance or a change in weather can cause a quick shift in elk movements or force animals to leave a locality overnight, so for elk hunting Lamicq uses portable stands that can be moved quickly to new locations.

The Nature of Elk Hunting

My good friend Rich LaRocco and I hunted elk together in Colorado. Rich had bowhunted for deer, but this was his first elk trip. We backpacked five miles and set up camp late one evening. The next morning we slogged through a boggy meadow and climbed a winding trail to emerge at timberline a mile above camp.

"Let's stop here and bugle before we get in the open," I suggested.

In the faint gray light of dawn I blew a long shrill whistle with my call. We stood silently, shivering. Within five seconds we heard an echoing whistle. It was a bull.

Staying in the trees, we circled below the bull, and an hour later, after several exploratory setups and some bugling, we sneaked within 100 yards of the elk. Rich set up out front to shoot and I hid behind a tree to bugle. As soon as I thrashed some brush and blew my call the bull shrieked threateningly and headed our way. Then he appeared, a huge animal, a dream bull, with antlers as thick as tree stumps. The rack swept back high and wide. During my 10 years of exhaustive elk hunting I'd seen dozens of bulls, but none compared with this animal.

I bugled violently, and the bull swaggered toward me. Rich tensed to draw his bow as the animal passed him at 30,

25, then 20 yards. Suddenly the elk stopped briefly, tested the air and then whirled and disappeared. Rich didn't get a shot, but we were both shaking from the enormity of the experience. What a bull! What a start for Rich.

We bugled all morning, and finally at 1 p.m. we located another bull whistling across a canyon. We made a long march to this animal and at 6 p.m. we bugled him in and Rich shot him at 20 yards. The bull didn't go far and Rich had a dandy 5-point bull his first day out.

The following year Rich hunted in Colorado again, and on the first day he bugled in a 4-point bull and nailed it. Two seasons, two days of hunting, three bulls bugled in, two bulls bagged. Some start.

DIFFERENT VIEWS

Expectations play a big role in the success of any hunting trip, and I think many hunters find themselves bewildered and disappointed with elk hunting because it doesn't meet their expectations. And is it any wonder? Beginning hunters know only what they hear and read. It's a natural law that hunters forget the bad parts of a hunt—the dull and boring hours, the anguish and desperation—to dwell on the positive, exciting and productive moments. They leave out the elkless days and build up every slight encounter with a bull, and their hunts end up sounding like ceaseless processions of excitement and adventure. Magazine stories read the same way. Editors don't buy stories about boredom and fatigue, so writers dwell on action and success. The end result is that neophytes who hear and read these stories develop a distorted view of elk hunting, and false expectations set them up for disappointment.

It's also misleading to base expectations on what you've learned from a deer-hunting background. Not only are elk generally fewer and farther between than deer, regardless of the region, but they generally live in more rugged, inaccessible country. Also, in my opinion, elk have better senses and are a little smarter, or at least spookier, than deer. In a nutshell, hunting elk simply takes more time, energy, and maybe skill, than deer hunting requires.

Harvest figures from "Colorado Big Game Harvest, 1980," illustrates that point. During general rifle season, elk hunters

Rich LaRocco killed this bull on his first day of bowhunting for elk. His perception of elk hunting might be different from that of a person who's hunted for three seasons without killing an elk.

had a 17 percent success rate, and they hunted an average of 28 days per animal killed; during general deer seasons hunters had 36 percent success, and they hunted an average of 11 days per deer killed. That comparison might not seem fair since those seasons fell after the rut, but early-season statistics for archers and muzzleloaders show the same disparity. Bowhunters had 12 percent success and hunted 69 days per elk killed; and they had 22 percent success and hunted 35 days per deer killed. For muzzleloaders on elk it was 14 percent success and 37 days per animal; on deer it was 24 percent success and 18 days per animal.

The statistics for bow and muzzleloaders are drawn from the early season when elk are in the rut and are most vulnerable, but when deer are not in rut; and these statistics come from a period when elk were at an all-time high and deer, as a result of severe winter weather, were at extreme lows. So the gap in hunting difficulty may be even greater than these data reflect.

A "TYPICAL" HUNT

Figures from a "typical" hunt might give you some idea of what to expect. Mind you, this hunt isn't totally representative. I've had much easier hunts and some a lot harder, and this one falls somewhere in the middle. It took place in northeast Oregon, and two friends, Larry Jones and Jim Brackenbury, and I had an outfitter drop-camp us far from the nearest road. This is steep country, and we hunted solely on foot. I kept accurate records of our daily hunting to compute mileages hiked and elevations climbed, and to record the number of elk we saw and heard.

Over a period of 14 actual hunting days, we each averaged hiking 9.5 miles per day, with a low of five miles and a high of 17. In that country the terrain is either up or down, never flat, so vertical distance is significant. We each hiked an average of 2,500 vertical feet per day, and on the toughest days we climbed and descended as much as 4,000 vertical feet. In total we saw 143 cows, calves and spike bulls and 21 three-point or larger bulls, and we heard 18 bulls bugling. On the average we saw six elk per individual hunting day, and we hunted 1.25 days for each bull seen and 1.5 days for each bull heard. We averaged hiking 1.5 individual miles for each elk seen, 11

We averaged hiking 9.5 miles a day with an average elevational climb of 2,500 feet. Are you in good enough shape to maintain that kind of a grind, day after day? Here Larry Jones is hunting for elk in Oregon.

miles for each bull seen, and 13 miles for each bull heard. On the best three days of hunting we saw 24, 19 and 15 elk, respectively, but on some days we saw no elk and on others we saw only one or two. One day we saw five bulls, and we heard four bugling one day, but on several days we neither saw nor heard a bull.

MOOD SWINGS

Raw statistics hint at the nature of elk hunting, but they don't necessarily tell the whole story. Elk hunting seems to have changes of mood that can perplex and eat at a hunter. One day raises you to exultation and the next leaves you gnashing your teeth with anguish. In Montana the hunting had been outstanding. For the first five days, we'd bugled in at least one bull every day. One morning at 11 a.m. I sat on a ridge between two creek canyons and all around me bulls got wound up and called back and forth. It was like sitting in a carnival with merry-go-round calliopes piping on all sides. From one spot I could hear at least six bulls, and by walking to the other side of the ridge I could hear two more. It was paradise.

That night a heavy wind came up and the next morning rain splattered through the forest. The wind harmonized with my soul and brought excitement. I rushed from camp, eager to hunt, to encounter the first bull of the day, knowing this would be a day to remember. For an hour I bugled confidently. As no bulls answered, my pace seemed to increase. The melodious, entrancing sound of bulls still rang through my head from previous days and an urgency to revive that, to hear it for real, drove me on. By noon I was nearly running through the forest, driven by mounting desperation, knowing that bull elk were all around me and were hearing my call, yet were not answering. I didn't stop for lunch or even sit down to rest, but marched on, covering 15 miles of terrain that I knew from previous days held a dozen or more bulls. That night after dark I trudged into camp, weary, soaked, perplexed. Where had they gone? I hadn't heard one bull.

That swing from hot to cold typifies elk hunting. I've seen similar breaks on most hunts. It could be caused by any number of things, but the cause doesn't matter. It happens. You have to expect it.

HIGHS AND LOWS

The nature of bugling heightens the ups and downs, too. In bugling the encounter with an animal is audible as well as visual, and that adds an emotional dimension absent from most other forms of hunting. Just the sound of a bull, maybe one you never see, can raise you to an emotional peak; and losing contact with that bull can drop you equally low.

In Idaho I'd bugled off the top of a ridge and heard a bull far below. Racing downhill for a half-mile, I moved in and set up. The bull bugled violently, and for half an hour I worked in until he was just across a shallow draw. I couldn't see him in the thick timber, but the magnitude of his bellering made clear he was no more than 50 yards away, and he was hot. I was confident of pulling this bull in and as we shrieked back and forth, my emotions climbed with the anticipation of seeing this violent monarch emerge from the shadows to confront me. I was shaking and tense, getting higher and higher.

Then for the first time in 30 minutes the bull didn't answer.

Statistics show that elk hunting is far more difficult and time-consuming than is deer hunting. For that reason you must have undying resolve. Here George Neal packs out the head of a bull killed in Oregon. Would you be smiling after an experience like this? (Photo courtesy Larry D. Jones)

I waited and bugled again. No answer. For 10 more minutes I bugled, but my calling degenerated from challenge to question: "Are you still there?" An immutable silence answered: "No." And my feelings sank as low as they'd just been high.

PREPARATION

The nature of elk hunting, with its physical and emotional demands, requires special preparation. One is physical conditioning. In hiking 9.5 miles a day, Jim, Larry and I did only the minimum we felt necessary to hunt effectively. That doesn't mean you must be able to hike like that day after day but if you can't you must adapt your methods to your ability. You might choose to take a stand or to still hunt slowly, and if you're happy with that, do it. But if you desire to bugle in a bull then you have to be prepared for the challenge, and I'd say the better shape you're in the better your chances. Success in elk hunting, or at least in bugling, is roughly proportional to physical conditioning.

To prepare for any hunt I jog four to eight miles a day and exercise to improve general muscle tone. This isn't to imply that you have to be Man Mountain Dean to hunt elk. A sustained hunting effort depends much more on stamina than size or strength. A good case in point is Shari Fraker, in her mid-40s, who stands 5-feet 5-inches tall and weighs 120 pounds. Her husband, Jim, hunts with firearms so Shari hunts by herself during the bow season. She stays out until she kills an elk. One year she camped and hunted alone 17 days before she bagged a spike bull. Her success (five elk in five seasons) shows that conditioning and desire are far more important in elk hunting than physical prowess. Fraker writes:

" To get in shape for hunting and packing out meat, about a month before the season I start wearing a backpack all day with rocks in it. I do dishes, run the vacuum, feed the animals, paint the chicken house and so forth with my backpack full of rocks, and each day I add a rock to increase the weight. In addition I lift dumbbells each day and run several miles a week.

" I used to shoot my bow three hours a day and was able to keep the arrows inside a paper plate consistently out to 60 yards, even though most all of my shots at elk have been closer than that, but apparently I overdid the shooting and

Some hunters let conditions govern their moods. When the sun is shining and the bulls are bugling and everything is hunky-dory, they do fine. But can they take it when things go sour? Here Gary Alt is having a great time in Colorado. Gary had a great time on rainy days too.

developed a severe case of tennis elbow. The doctor advised me not to hunt that year, probably figuring I wouldn't really object to not going, but as far as I was concerned it was the end of the world. I bawled around the house for two weeks and Jim was about ready to divorce me. Well, I went hunting despite what the doctor said and got an elk and a deer, too. When the doctor found out that I went hunting anyway and that it was a big thing to me, he sent me to a physical therapist who works with athletes, and he put me on an exercise program to work my arm back into shape. Now I'm only able to shoot 15 to 30 minutes a day. Must get with it. Only 78 days till elk season!''

MENTAL CONDITIONING

Understanding the nature of elk hunting is a big step toward mental preparation. Expectations simply must be realistic. Elk hunting can place such strain on the mind and body that it can't be taken too seriously. If you've hunted all

Could you keep smiling even when you're sopping wet and haven't heard a bull all day? I managed a little smile for the camera, despite the conditions. No, I'm not cooking lunch, just trying to dry my soaking-wet socks. (Photo courtesy Larry D. Jones)

day without hearing or seeing an elk and you've walked so far your chin is dragging the ground, you have to remember that it's not the end of the world. It's just a part of the joy of hunting. You know that as soon as you've had a filling supper of freeze-dried gruel and a solid three hours of sleep, you'll be eager to rise before dawn to do the same thing all over again.

Some hunters let conditions govern their moods. On sunny days when bulls are bugling and everything is hunky-dory, they smile and joke and generally love elk hunting; but when the rain starts and their clothes slosh with every step and elk seem to go underground, their smiles disappear and talk turns from hunting to going home.

To be a good elk hunter, you must have undying resolve. My friend Larry Jones exemplifies the perfect elk-hunting attitude. Larry always carries meat sacks, and every day he prepares meticulously from camouflage to broadheads to footwear, because every time he leaves camp he expects to kill a bull. He never entertains the thought that he might not succeed, and even when things go wrong, he shrugs it off and gets right back to hunting. He knows no discouragement, no quitting, no defeat.

Attitudes can permeate a hunting camp. Expressions of despair and failure can tear it apart, and displays of determination and enthusiasm can fire it up. For that reason I think not only preparing yourself mentally but choosing hunting partners is vital to elk-hunting success. I won't hunt with persons who are easily discouraged, because they may break my resolve. At the same time I realize that the hunting-partner relationship is reciprocal, and that I must contribute, too. For that reason I've eliminated two words—"discouraged" and "depressed"—from my vocabulary. Given the demanding nature of elk hunting, these feelings, if allowed to germinate, can encompass and destroy a hunt.

THE END OF A DREAM

To cap these thoughts on the nature of elk hunting, let me tell you about one of my greatest elk hunts. Ken Barr and I loaded up two backpacks apiece, and leapfrogged them nine miles into an Oregon wilderness. We planned to hunt for two weeks. I'd hunted this country before and had killed a couple of cow elk there, but never a bull, and my dream, the focus of my hunting life, was to take a bull elk from that country. Then I'd be satisfied, my dream fulfilled. This was the year.

We set up camp at timberline and began to hunt familiar basins, and we found elk. One morning we bugled in a feisty five-point and I missed a close shot, and another day in the same basin, we bugled in two small bulls, but we hadn't set up well enough and the bulls sensed our presence and milled around at 80 yards for an hour, hollering at us and peering, but never coming within good bow range.

Another evening we slipped within 75 yards of a bull with cows, and he rushed our way with a full head of steam. Then he caught our scent on a swirling wind and vanished silently.

The weather stayed warm and beautiful. The camping was great and I shot a buck, but with the dry weather, elk kegged up tight and for days on end we scarcely saw an animal.

As the days wore on and warm weather persisted and the action failed to pick up, I began to push harder, feeling that the dream was slipping from my fingers. I scoured every basin and bench and canyon and pocket that I knew, but it seemed the harder I hunted, the scarcer the elk became. I cussed the weather and the elk and prayed and pulled my hair, trying to find a combination that would produce a dream bull, but at the end of two weeks, 14 full days of hard hunting, I sat at the head of a huge canyon, meadows spread out directly below giving way to miles of black timber, and watched the last day of the season come to a close. Black clouds, the first imperfections we'd seen in blue sky for 14 days, billowed up the canyon and cast a dark gloom over the mountains. Rain was coming. But it was too late. The hunt was over and my dream had died. Unfulfilled. My heart was sick. Why did it have to end this way? Why couldn't I get an elk? I'd tried hard, oh, how I'd tried. Could I have hiked farther, looked sharper, listened more closely, hunted more wisely? I didn't know. I'd tried. Yet I'd failed.

The nature of elk hunting? You figure it out. Maybe it's two bulls in two days. Maybe it's two weeks of hard labor yielding nothing but the satisfaction of knowing you've tried. That's what elk hunting is like. Or something like that.

Camping and Gear

My first wilderness elk hunt left an indelible mark on me. Two friends and I backpacked 11 miles into the deep wilderness of eastern Oregon in mid-September when the sun was shining and deep dust carpeted the trails. It was a glorious time to be outdoors and we anticipated a memorable, romantic backcountry adventure, a real mountain-man experience. Can you blame us for being elated?

That first night rain began to fall. The next day we all got wet but that was only a minor discomfort. Rain made the woods smell good and we could simply dry our clothes when the sun came out and we'd be no worse for the experience. But the rain didn't stop. It continued the next day and the next, and for eight days rain fell continuously until every item of camp gear and clothing we owned was soaking wet. About mid-week, snow started to fall on the highest peaks and each morning the snow line crept farther down the mountains until it lay just above camp. At first only our hunting effectiveness was hampered because in our misery we functioned poorly, but as the snow drew closer to our creekbottom camp and piled up to a depth of 15 inches, we began to fear for our survival. Finally on the ninth day we decided to get out.

In planning any elk hunt, make sure you have adequate shelter. You can count on lousy weather any time you're in elk country. This hunter has set up a lean-to shelter made out of a large plastic tarp. (Photo courtesy of Larry D. Jones.)

To say the least our dreams were shattered, but under the circumstances it seemed our only choice. Hiking out that afternoon we bulled through 20 inches of snow on the pass that separated our camp from our car, and the tough going there only confirmed that retreating was the smart thing to do. At the same time, doubts gnawed at my mind. Surely at this time of year the snow wouldn't last long. If we could have stuck it out just a little longer the snow might have melted and we'd have got out okay. And even as we hiked the last couple of miles to the car, the sky seemed to be clearing. A cold chill pervaded the air, and not the damp unfriendly hypothermia chill we'd endured the previous nine days but an honest-to-goodness frosty cold that meant clear skies and beautiful sunny weather. Something told me we'd blown it.

That night we stayed in a flophouse hotel in a nearby town. The walls of the musty, bleak room were papered with cheap calendar pictures of high-country scenes, the country we'd just escaped from, as if the previous occupant had tried vicariously to capture the glory we'd been seeking in the wilderness. After a terrible night's sleep we got up to peer out the dirty window at a spotless azure sky, and the mountains where we'd just been, alluring and full of adventure, gleamed white and pure against the distant blue horizon. We knew the elk we'd seen there, the two bulls jousting in a meadow, the herd bull chasing his harem of 20 cows, would be bugling and that the backcountry there now would hold all of the adventure that we'd longed to experience. That moment, looking at those bright mountains full of bugling elk, knowing I'd left it all behind because I'd come ill-prepared, ranks as the low point of my hunting career. I vowed at that moment that I would never be forced to quit a hunt again because of conditions, and that I'd never again hunt at less than my highest level as a result of lack of knowledge or planning. So far I've upheld that vow, and here are some of the things that have helped me do it.

THE HUNTING PACK

Elk hunting can lead you a long way from camp into merciless country and in miserable weather. I've always thought mountain climbers are crazy because they purposely place themselves in dangerous circumstances, but in a way elk hunters do the same thing. The isolation and rugged terrain that an elk hunter seeks combined with commonly terrible weather can produce life-threatening conditions for the hunter who isn't prepared.

In addition, the very best moments of the day, the premium hunting times, are those first and last minutes of daylight, but all too often we miss those times as we're hurrying to and from camp, afraid we might get caught in the dark. To hunt efficiently by utilizing those prime moments, we must go prepared to cope with darkness and other hazards involved with hunting the grey edges of day. In part that involves knowing the country so you can find your way, but it also means having along the equipment to deal with darkness and emergencies. One year, on a backcountry hunt with my friend Ken Barr, I spent more time wandering around in the dark than in daylight, yet I felt comfortable doing it; it had become part of the hunt. That was quite a revolution for someone inherently afraid of the dark, but through knowledge of the country and confidence in my

Hunting packs generally come in two forms: the rucksack and the fanny pack. Whatever your choice of pack it must be comfortable and lightweight, and it must go into the field with you every time you leave camp.

equipment, I'd cast off any fears and roamed the country with confidence, day or night. That's the kind of confidence needed for efficient hunting.

A daypack is the heart of confident hunting and to be of value a pack must be comfortable and convenient. If it's not you'll end up leaving it in camp half the time where it will do no good. Bowhunter Doug Kittredge learned this lesson the hard way in Arizona. It was the first day of the season and rain was falling hard, so he and his companions decided they'd just walk out for a quick look around, then return to camp for breakfast. Nothing serious. Kittredge left his hunting pack in camp. Not far away the hunters heard a bull bugling; then they spotted a huge bull with a harem of cows. They pursued the herd, which led them more than a mile from camp, then they bugled the bull within range and Kittredge shot it. This was about noon. The bull led them on a long chase and they followed until dark. Then they headed back toward camp, but a heavy fog set in and they ended up walking in circles and finally resigned themselves to sleeping in the mud under a juniper tree. One of them had a half dozen matches in his pocket and after several tense tries they managed to start a fire, which may have saved their lives. Kittredge said that by then he was exhausted and because he'd been wet all day, he'd begun to shiver uncontrollably in the cold night air. He believes that if they hadn't got that fire going he well could have died of hypothermia, a condition that results when the inner body temperature drops. If he'd had his survival pack along, which contained a compass, reliable fire-building materials, shelter and extra clothing, he either would have found his way back to camp, or at least would have been able to spend a comfortable night in the field. That near-disaster started out as a mere half-hour looksee walk from camp. Never leave camp without your hunting pack and survival gear.

Hunting packs generally come in two forms: rucksack or fanny pack. I personally find the weight of a rucksack on my shoulders all day very tiring, so I prefer a fanny pack. That's a matter of personal preference, so get what best suits you. The equipment you carry also can be an individual choice, but I consider some items essential in all hunting. One is a flashlight. Mine is a small light about 6 inches long that takes two AA batteries, and along with the light I carry two fresh

Some items are essential for all hunting, such as flashlight, map and compass, and first-aid kit. My hunting pack also includes a lightweight plastic tarp for building an emergency shelter such as this small A-frame shelter made of long branches and plastic. I spent a comfortable night here, despite heavy rain.

batteries and a spare bulb. As a safety measure, I always turn one battery backwards so that the light can't get turned on inside my pack and burn out the batteries.

Map and compass must be included in any hunting pack along with reliable fire-starting materials. In addition I carry a lightweight plastic, 9'x12' tarp to build emergency shelter, and on several occasions I've set up an A-frame made of long branches and covered it with that plastic to create a comfortable overnight home in the field. Also my pack contains a small first aid kit, a needle and thread for patching torn clothes, a knife, small saw, and cheesecloth bags for meat care. Appendix D contains a complete list of items that go into my hunting pack.

CLOTHING

Clothing contributes greatly to your hunting effectiveness and staying power in the field. If I had only one word to sum up the perfect clothing for elk hunting, I'd say "wool." I think that's true under most conditions, but it's particularly applicable on a backpack hunt where you're limited in the amount of clothing you can carry. In a big horse camp or car camp you can take lightweight cotton clothes for warm weather, long underwear, a heavy jacket, wool—an unlimited amount of clothing to meet all conditions—but in backpacking one set of clothing has to cover all situations. Wool bridges the gap between warm and cold weather, dry and wet, better than most other materials.

I recall one particularly rainy hunt during which I gave up on raingear and consigned myself to getting wet as I slogged through dripping brush. My clothes were soaked constantly for more than a week. Early morning presented the real ordeal, and I almost had to laugh as I hid in my sleeping bag and peeked out at that sopping heap of clothes lying there like a Labrador retriever fresh out of the water. The thought of pulling on those clammy clothes made getting out of the sleeping bag doubly hard, but once it was done the clothes, like magic, became warm and comfortable. That's because they were all wool.

Wool is soft and pliable under all conditions. It feels good on those frosty mornings that accompany all elk hunting, it doesn't get clammy even on warm days when you start sweating, and it's the best material in damp weather. When cotton gets wet, for example, it holds a layer of moisture right against the skin, which cools you through the processes of conduction and evaporation. Nothing is more clammy and uncomfortable than damp cotton clothing. In contrast, wool wicks moisture away from the skin, which allows an insulating layer of air to form, and as a result wool will keep you warm even when it's damp.

In addition wool is always soft and quiet, which contributes to hunting stealth. Even the softest cotton, especially if it's wet, scratches against brush. To carry quietness to its full extent make a wool cover for your hunting pack, because nylon, the material used in most packs, makes a terrible racket in the brush.

Raingear has to be the worst-possible garment for hunting, but in a downpour it can really save you. For that reason, whenever threatening weather promises heavy rain, I carry a very light, rubberized nylon parka in my fanny pack.

FOOTWEAR

One year while hunting with two friends I wore rugged and comfortable insulated leather boots that protected my feet well. One day one of my partners, who's not particularly known for tact, said, "If Dwight doesn't get rid of those clodhopper boots, I'm going to cut his feet off. Clomp, clomp, clomp!"

That didn't exactly bolster my self-image, but it certainly got my attention and forced me to think about footwear. The biggest problem with those boots, at slightly over 3 pounds apiece, was weight. It's often said that 1 pound on the feet is equal to 5 pounds on the back. If that's true—I can't support it scientifically—then wearing a pair of boots that weighs 6 pounds, compared to a pair that weighs 2 pounds, equals putting 20 extra pounds in your hunting pack. Would anybody in his right mind carry 20 unneeded pounds?

The point is that eliminating weight on your feet saves energy; you'll go a lot farther in a day with less effort. Just as important you can move a lot quieter and faster in lightweight footwear. That may not make a lot of difference when you're covering ground to locate a bull, but when you get in close and have to stick and move, playing cat and mouse at close range, it could make the difference between success and failure. The lighter and quieter your footwear the more quickly you can move with stealth.

Friends of mine hunt in running or tennis shoes and they seem to get along fine, but these kinds of shoes offer little foot protection in rough, rocky country. I prefer a compromise. Many companies these days make what they call "hiking shoes," which incorporate nylon and leather into rugged backcountry footgear. I have a pair made by Nike that has traveled more than 500 miles of tough terrain, and it's still going strong. I think this style of rugged but lightweight shoe is a good choice for elk hunting.

The one problem you'll run into, if you're hunting in boggy country or during rainy weather, is wet feet. Many new lightweight hiking shoes and boots contain Gore-Tex, a waterproof material that some companies claim makes their boots and shoes waterproof. I've used three different brands of Gore-Tex hiking boots and shoes, and none has even lived close to that claim. It may take the water a little longer to get into these shoes than into canvas tennis shoes, but it does get in. Many companies also make "waterproof" leather boots, and indeed some are water repellent, but here again I've owned several pairs and none could stand up to the test of a good rainy day. The upshot is that I now opt for light weight and comfort and resign myself to getting wet feet. Nylon shoes dry quickly, and with dry socks in camp, I can always start each day with dry feet.

A good alternative in miserably wet conditions is the rubber-bottom, leather-upper boot, such as L.L. Bean's Maine Hiking shoe. With an insole to protect your feet from rock bruises, these are comfortable and fairly lightweight, and they'll keep your feet dry.

BACKPACKING

Wilderness. When most of us dream about elk hunting we dream about wilderness, so let's first look at some ways to hunt wilderness country. The most rudimentary is backpacking. It's often assumed that you must have horses to hunt wilderness elk, and horses do have their place, but that doesn't mean you can't hunt without them. Some serious elk hunters purposely leave their horses at home at times. Ron

I personally wouldn't consider backpacking more than 3 to 4 miles if it involved packing out an entire elk by myself, but with partners that distance can be increased as long as the partners are willing to spend their time packing meat. Here Gary Alt (left) helps Rich LaRocco pack up a load of meat off Rich's bull.

On my "dream" hunt, Ken Barr (left) and I loaded up two packs apiece and leapfrogged them into the back country. Even all of this preparation couldn't guarantee us an elk, and my dream failed to come true. Is that the real nature of elk hunting?

Granneman owns horses specifically for elk hunting, but he doesn't always use them. Some of his hunting areas are fairly restricted and he must camp close to where he'll hunt. In these cases his horses must graze the same meadows that elk might be using, which could disturb the very game he plans to hunt, so in these cases Granneman backpacks and leaves his horses at home. Don Rajnus, a rancher in Oregon, has horses at his disposal, but he backpacks for elk. Rajnus figures taking care of horses while he's hunting is more trouble than it's worth. When he gets an elk down he hires a local packer to haul it out of the backcountry for him.

And that's something you have to consider. It's a rare individual who can backpack an elk any great distance. I'll discuss meat care thoroughly in Chapter 10 but for now just remember that the meat off an average bull, in the quarters, weighs about 400 pounds, and you can add to that the weight of head, antlers and hide, plus all of your camp gear. Assuming you can pack 100 pounds, which is unlikely, you'd have to make a minimum of five round trips to pack out that animal and your camp. That task pretty well limits the distance you can backpack; at least it does if you plan to carry the meat out yourself. I personally wouldn't consider backpacking more than 3 to 4 miles if I planned to do my own meat packing. Of course, that distance can be extended if your hunting partners will help pack meat. In Colorado, three of us packed Rich LaRocco's bull 9 miles. That arrangement means your hunting partners have to sacrifice their hunting time to pack meat so you'd better discuss that little detail before someone kills an elk.

That doesn't mean backpacking is limited to short distances, but if you're going farther, you must make provisions for meat care. In most cases that means you arrange for a local packer or outfitter to bring in his horses once you've killed an animal, but line up these services ahead of the hunt. Some outfitters won't do this kind of work, and you could get stuck with an elk 10 miles from a road and no way to retrieve it. I've backpacked as far as 15 miles and have had no problems with meat spoilage, but I've always arranged for packing services ahead of time. The price for packing out an elk generally runs from $200 to $400, depending on the distance and time involved for the packer.

Planning a backpack hunt is a subject unto itself and goes beyond the scope of this book, but one aspect of backpacking deserves special attention. Even during the early season you can count on unmerciful weather. It's been a rare trip on which I haven't been snowed on or rained on or both. For that reason I give shelter some special thought. The trip described at the beginning of this chapter was a disaster largely because of poor shelter. After our clothing got wet we had no way to dry it. Our little tents weren't large enough for clothes lines, and we couldn't hang clothes outside because of the continuous rain. To compound the misery, each night as we dragged in after dark from hunting, we struggled to light a soggy heap of ashes we wryly called a fire and stood around in the driving rain, trying to scrape together some kind of dinner. It was strictly an exercise in the will to survive.

In contrast, on an equally rainy, drizzly hunt in Montana, Larry Jones and I set up a dependable two-man tent for sleeping, then we made a large lean-to out of a 12' by 16'

It's a rare individual who can backpack an elk any great distance, so know your limitations. My upper limit for backpacking an elk is about 3 to 4 miles. Here Ken Barr hauls an elk quarter out of the backcountry.

plastic tarp. We supported the front edge of the tarp over a pole tied between two trees 10 feet off the ground, then we staked the other end of the tarp to the ground. We put our fire pit at the front edge of the lean-to, and we stacked dry wood under the shelter. Each night when we returned from hunting, we immediately lit a blazing fire. Then we sat in comfort out of the rain and cooked our dinner and told stories. We didn't just endure camp life; we enjoyed it. Each day we hung wet socks and underwear under the lean-to so we'd have dry clothes at the end of the day. After trying many different arrangements, I now consider minimum shelter for a backpacking camp to be a waterproof tent for sleeping and a lean-to shelter for protection from rain and snow during the day. Plastic makes a good lean-to, but a tarp made of waterproof rip-stop nylon is more durable.

THE DROP CAMP

Some dedicated elk hunters buy their own horses strictly

The drop camp is a feasible intermediate step for most of us between backpacking and the fully outfitted hunt. With a drop camp you enjoy the use of pack stock and a comfortable camp, yet you can hunt on your own and you pay less than for a guided hunt.

for hunting. In ways that's ideal because you have the freedom to hunt when and how you want, and you're not restricted by distance as you are in backpacking. If you have acreage near home you can keep horses there, or as one hunting acquaintance suggests, you can board horses with ranchers in states where you plan to hunt. For the person who lives to do nothing but hunt elk, buying horses is reasonable, but for most of us it's not practical. Keeping a couple of horses year around costs more than hiring a packer to accommodate a once-a-year elk hunt, and unless you're a real horse person, having horses on an elk hunt can be a major pain in the neck. More than once I've run into frustrated hunters who've spent a day or two of good hunting time looking for lost horses or doctoring injured stock.

That brings up a more feasible alternative for most of us, the drop camp, which is an intermediary step between backpacking and taking a fully outfitted and guided hunt. In a drop camp you enjoy many of the benefits of an outfitted hunt, such as the use of horses to pack gear and meat into and out of the backcountry and you have a roomy, comfortable camp with plenty of food and good shelter. In contrast, you hunt on your own and the cost is much less. Some outfitters will pack in your gear and drop it off for you and you set up everything yourself. Others prefer to set up their own tents and provide all the camp gear and food for you. Several years ago two friends and I took such a hunt. The outfitter set up three wall tents, two for sleeping, one for cooking; split firewood; provided all cooking utensils, stoves and gas; and made a meat check at the end of the first week. Then he packed out game and our personal gear at the end of the second week. Total cost for that service at that time was $600, or $200 apiece. It would be more now.

That all sounds ideal, and it's a great way to hunt, but just like most things in life, drop-camp hunting has its shortcomings. If an outfitter is running guided hunts at the same time, chances are good he won't set you up in the midst of his finest hunting country where he's going to be working with guided hunters. Also, if he has other drop-camp parties he could set up several groups in one drainage, which could ruin the hunting for everybody. In elk hunting you need plenty of elbow room. If you live far away and don't know the country you're pretty much at the mercy of the outfitter, so try to get some guarantees. All of my drop-camp hunting has taken place in familiar country, so I've told the outfitter exactly where to place my camp. That's the ideal way to operate if you know where you want to hunt.

Also understand the packer's services. On the hunt mentioned above the packer was supposed to supply gas for the stoves, but he "forgot." At the end of the first week he picked up a deer I'd shot, which he promised to get into cold storage in a nearby town, but when we came out at the end of two weeks—a warm, rainy two weeks—the deer was hanging in a screened meat shed at the packer's lodge. I could smell it 50 yards away. Fortunately some liberal trimming got rid of the mold and little meat was lost, but the fact is that the packer didn't do what he'd said he would. Make sure you've ironed out such details before the hunt.

Another drawback to the drop-camp hunt, say opposed to backpacking, is that you're stuck in a central location. If you're in good shape you can continue to hike out in ever enlarging circles, or you can rent horses from your outfitter.

Not all elk live in deep wilderness. The fact is that you might hunt more efficiently in regions with roads. Here Gary Alt prepares to hunt a canyon in northwest Colorado.

Or you can try a third approach called bivouacking.

BIVOUAC HUNTING

In bivouac hunting you carry the necessities for living on your back. Your home is where you're standing at the moment, so you can head out cross-country without looking back. Although a bivouac pack weighs more than a regular hunting pack, in the long run you save energy because there's no wasted effort in hiking to and from camp in the mornings and evenings. And you hunt more efficiently because when you come to a great spot you can hunt right there through the last few minutes of daylight, and you can start hunting again at dawn without a long trudge out from camp in the dark.

A regular frame pack doesn't work in bivouac hunting because the rigid frame restricts your movement, and if it protrudes above your shoulders it continually snags on limbs and branches. A bivouac pack must have a low profile and it must be flexible to become a welcome part of your body. My bivouac pack consists of two parts, a large fanny pack and a rucksack. When loaded the fanny pack supports the rucksack to take weight off my shoulders, just as a padded hip belt does on a frame pack.

A bivouac pack also must be light. For me, 15 pounds is about the maximum. The fanny pack contains all of my regular hunting-pack items. Into the rucksack I stuff a lightweight down sleeping bag, and between the two packs I strap a small, waterproof Gore-Tex tent called a Bivvy Sack, which is made by SierraWest of Santa Barbara, California. It weighs just over 2 pounds. The only extra clothing that goes into this pack is a change of socks.

Food limits the number of days you can bivouac. Figure on about 1 pound of food for each day you hunt. Because of the weight and bulk of food I rarely bivouac for more than two to three nights. Simplicity characterizes my bivouac menu: Pre-bagged granola cereal with dry milk for breakfast (just add water); pre-rolled tortillas with cheese or beans for lunch; freeze-dried dinner at night (just pour boiling water into the container). The only gear you need for preparing these meals is a small aluminum pot, a spoon, and a small gas or Sterno stove. In country with plenty of water for putting our fires, I often forget the stove and cook over a fire at night and eat the other meals cold. In addition to these meals I carry gorp (mixed raisins, nuts and chocolate candies) and two or three pieces of jerky for each day. Bivouac hunting can be combined with any other type of camping—backpacking, drop camp, or car camping.

ROAD HUNTING

Elk generally are described as wilderness animals, but don't be fooled into thinking you have to hunt roadless backcountry to enjoy good elk hunting. The fact is that you might hunt more effectively in regions with roads. The reason is mobility. Let's face it, in the backcountry you can hunt only as far and wide as you can hike on foot or ride on horseback. By car camping and hunting off roads, you can effectively cover a much greater territory in a given amount of time. In any elk hunting finding animals is the name of the game and road hunting lends itself to this aspect of hunting. "Road hunting" doesn't mean that you drive roads looking or bugling for elk; rather you drive to a good location and hike out from there. If you don't find elk in that location, then the next day you try a different drainage or mountain. And don't feel deprived if you're stuck hunting near roads. The four largest elk ever taken by bowhunters—at the time of this writing—where killed by car-camping hunters.

A road camp can be as simple or as elaborate as you want to make it. If camping comfort means something to you then set up a big permanent camp with wall tents and drive out from there each day. For greater mobility camp light, using your car as a base of operations. That way you can quickly pack up and move on if you find yourself in a poor area.

Jay Elmer's concern in camping is to avoid spooking animals that he's hunting. His party agrees on a central meeting place far from the hunting area. Each day the hunters meet there at noon for a big meal and storytelling. Then in the afternoon each drives his separate way for the evening hunt. Jay hunts until dark then eats a quick meal right there, throws out his sleeping bag next to his car and goes to bed. He builds no fires and does no talking or carousing. The next morning he hunts early then about noon returns to the central meeting place where he and his friends gather for another big meal and socializing.

CAMP LOCATION

This brings up an important consideration in camping. Elk react strongly to human disturbance; if they're bothered they'll move out. For that reason always avoid putting your camp where it will disturb the animals you're hunting. In general, place camp at least a mile from where you plan to hunt. In foot hunting such as backpacking you might want to camp closer to eliminate as much dead walking as possible each day, but in that case, camp so that a ridge or rim separates you from the elk to buffer the sounds and smells of camp. And camp in an inconspicuous spot where animals can't see you from a distance, and keep noise to a minimum. If you're bivouacking in the midst of elk, be very quiet and don't build a fire.

Try to camp efficiently. That's particularly important in the backcountry where you want to economize on movement. Billy Cruise, who's killed many elk with a bow, owns his own horses. The first day he packs clear to the far side of his hun-

No, that's not a caveman reincarnate, it's simply Larry Jones after a long day of hunting. In Montana Larry and I set up a comfortable camp with a tent for sleeping and a lean-to shelter for additional protection. Each night when we returned from hunting, we immediately lit a blazing fire and sat near it in comfort, out of the rain, as we ate dinner and told stories.

ting territory; then he progressively hunts back toward his vehicle. In backpacking, plan an itinerary where you can hunt a radius of two miles or so from your first camp then pack up and move four miles to hunt another two-mile radius and so forth. Plan a systematic route so you don't waste valuable time and energy retracing your steps.

And place your camp with an escape route in mind. On that first wilderness elk hunt described earlier, my friends and I hadn't thought about that, and that's why we had to retreat. We'd boxed ourselves in so that we had to cross a high pass through deep snow to get out. If we'd looked for alternatives before the hunt we could have stayed without concern. And that's the point; think ahead. If you plan your camp and gear with care, you'll hunt efficiently and you'll stay to the glorious end every time.

Early-season hunting presents special meat-care problems. Oregon bowhunter George Neal knows he has to take care of this animal quickly to prevent meat spoilage. (Photo courtesy of Larry D. Jones.)

Meat Care

Early-season hunting presents special meat-care problems. Clem Stechelin, a meat processor in Oregon, said that during the 1982 bow season, which ran from late August through September, hunters brought four elk to his plant for processing that were spoiled and inedible. As you would expect, he couldn't do much with those animals. The only thing that could have saved them was proper field care.

Heat is the major threat to meat in the early season. If you can't get an elk cooled quickly, and keep it cool, then the meat will sour. The thick hide of an elk holds in body heat, and warm early-season weather slows the cooling rate of meat, so the early-season hunter must take special steps to cool an elk quickly. Another problem unique to the early season is flies. As soon as an elk hits the ground in September blow flies show up by the thousands, and if you're not prepared to keep them off you'll end up packing more fly eggs out of the backcountry than meat.

Other threats to meat, which aren't necessarily unique to the early season, are contamination and moisture. Dirt of any kind introduces bacteria that sour meat fast, and lingering moisture, such as a pool of blood or rainwater trapped next to meat, enhances bacterial growth and speeds up spoilage.

SHOULD YOU SKIN AN ELK?

It should go without saying that before anything else you field dress your animal, that is, remove all internal organs, including the wind pipe and esophagus. Then comes the question of whether to skin the animal immediately or to leave the hide on. Professor Ray Field, at the University of Wyoming, has studied this question extensively, and he's found good reasons for leaving the hide on an animal. Field said that meat under the hide is virtually sterile; no meat-souring bacteria are present, so leaving the hide on can slow the rate of spoilage. Also, the hide prevents excessive drying, which gives you juicier meat. In addition hide left on meat acts as insulation to keep meat cool during the day. In his studies Field found that if meat was cooled quickly, leaving the hide on in no way affects flavor or tenderness. In a nutshell, Field recommends that you leave the hide on if, within a day, you can get your elk to a cooler where it can be skinned under clean conditions, or if the air temperature is dropping below freezing so the meat will cool quickly at night. Field does warn that even in cold weather you must split an elk into halves down the backbone with an ax or saw and hang the animal to allow good air circulation. The thick hide on an elk insulates like a down sleeping bag, and anywhere the hide is pressed against the ground the meat won't cool, even in the coldest weather.

HEAT

As you may have guessed you'll rarely find those conditions during August and September, so I would say as a general rule that early-season hunters must skin elk immediately. Clem Stechelin said that most soured meat he's seen has resulted because hunters didn't get the hides off their animals fast enough. In some cases that's been because of ignorance; they didn't realize the importance of fast skinning. In other cases hunters simply didn't find their animals in time. Stechelin said that a couple of soured elk brought into his shop had been shot late in the evening but weren't recovered until the following morning. You can just about bet money that if an elk lays overnight you'll lose the meat. That's why it's particularly important to prepare to stay

Assuming you'll find yourself in the field with an elk that must be butchered immediately, always carry the equipment needed to work on an elk by yourself. Nobody can handle an elk in one piece, so plan to dissect that animal into manageable parts, as George Neal is doing here.

overnight in the field. Bowhunters in particular often must trail animals some distance after a shot. Always have a good flashlight along so you can trail an animal after dark, and if you're car camping and hit an animal in the evening, go back to camp and get your gas lantern. You'll find that you can follow a blood trail very well at night with artificial light. And don't give up until you've found the animal. Otherwise, in most cases you can kiss it goodbye.

But don't give up just because you don't find an animal within a couple of hours. Look until you're fully convinced there's simply no hope. One year I shot a cow elk late in the evening and trailed it quickly for a half-hour until dark. Then I trailed by flashlight and made slow but steady progress for four hours, when my flashlight batteries gave out—that's one reason for carrying spare batteries. The next morning I resumed the search at daylight and finally found the elk at 11 a.m., 17 hours after I'd hit it. Judging from the position of the hit and the condition of the animal, I'd say the elk had died shortly after the shot. The first thing I noticed was that a bear had beat me to the elk and had eaten 20 to 30 pounds of meat off the rump. That may have been a blessing in disguise, because it turned out that there wasn't a sour piece of meat on that entire animal; it was delicious. I suspect that just enough body heat had dissipated through the hole made by the bear to keep the meat from spoiling. Never give up on an animal as long as there's hope of finding it.

Even if you do skin an animal quickly, you're not necessarily in the clear. You have to assure that the meaty, thick portions, particularly on a big bull, cool properly. Major problem areas are the hip sockets and front shoulders, which are the meatiest, thickest parts of an elk. Stechelin said he's seen bones in these areas on improperly cooled elk turn almost black, and spoilage has spread out rapidly from there. He said he often pokes a knife deep into the hip sockets to allow heat to dissipate. I've found that it's a good idea to open up the hams and front shoulders to allow quick cooling. When Rich LaRocco killed a large bull in Colorado,we gutted the animal immediately and had it completely skinned, quartered and laid out on rocks before midnight. The next morning heavy frost coated the meadows, and puddles of water were iced over, yet Rich's bull wasn't fully cooled out. Next to the leg bones in the hams the meat was still warm with body heat. We had no problem with spoilage on that elk, but that incident definitely impressed on us the need, even in cold weather, to open up heavy portions to assure quick cooling. Good air circulation is essential for quick cooling, so always get meat off the ground. The ideal solution is to hang it in the shade where a cool breeze can blow around it, but if you're alone and aren't strong enough to hang the heavy shoulders and hams by yourself, at least prop them against rocks or lay them over logs where air can swirl around them.

Dirt is always a problem in the field. Any contamination enhances the growth of bacteria and speeds up meat spoilage, so go out of your way to keep meat as clean as possible. When you skin an elk leave fat on to protect meat from dirt and to prevent drying. Shot-up areas will be the first to spoil because of moisture and contamination, so trim these areas clean and wash the meat thoroughly. (Washing presents no moisture problems as long as you assure good air circulation to dry the meat later.) And as soon as you've skinned your animal bag it in cloth sacks to keep off dirt and flies.

That's why you always carry meat sacks as you're hunting.

ON YOUR OWN

Handling an elk under any conditions is no easy task, but hunting with partners and near roads can certainly ease the burden somewhat. If you're near a road you may be able to winch your elk into a tree where you can skin it in one piece, or possibly you can load an entire field-dressed animal into your truck to haul to a meat-processing plant. Some hunters use chain saw winches to slide whole elk from the bottoms of canyons up to roads. Those situations are ideal.

But if your hunting goes like mine, you'll end up by yourself in some bottomless pit of a canyon or on a distant mountain where the nearest road is five miles away. That's when you learn how to handle an elk. Let's look at some figures. During studies in Wyoming the average field dressed (gutted) weight of six bull elk was 437 pounds and of six cow elk 339 pounds. Using weight-conversion figures derived from these studies the average live weight of the bulls would have been 647 pounds and of the cows 500 pounds. That was the average for elk ranging in age from 2 to 9 years old. Mature bulls were found to weigh about 770 pounds on the hoof and 521 field dressed. (You can figure out the weight of your elk from the accompanying conversion chart from Bulletin 594, Agricultural Experiment Station, University of Wyoming, Laramie, WY 82071.) You can see from those figures that you won't toss an elk around the way you might the average deer.

Let's assume you're alone, you've just killed an elk far from any roads, and the weather is warm. You have to get that animal gutted, skinned and cooled immediately. Assuming you'll find yourself in this position some day, always carry the equipment needed to work on that ungainly critter. Here's my basic equipment: 50 feet of nylon cord; knife and small steel or stone for sharpening the knife; small folding saw; game bags; small flashlight. Why a flashlight for butchering an elk? If you shoot an animal in the evening you'll end up skinning well into the night. A fire provides poor working light, so I carry a flashlight that can be held in my teeth; it assures direct light right where I'm working.

If it's a big bull chances are you can't move it to an ideal

Weight conversion figures for bull elk.

Weight example	Factor
Whole weight = 592 lb.[a]	$1.48 \times$ field dressed weight
Field dressed weight = 400 lb. (viscera removed)	$0.675 \times$ whole weight
Clean dressed weight = 332 lb. (skin and head removed)	$0.83 \times$ field dressed weight
Packaged retail cuts = 216 lb. (bone left in leg, loin, rib and shoulder cuts)	$0.54 \times$ field dressed weight
Packaged cuts (all boneless) = 172 lb.	$0.43 \times$ field dressed weight

[a] Whole weight is used in place of live weight. Whole weight is slightly less than live weight because it does not take into account blood loss at the time of kill. Blood loss on slaughtered steers ranges from 3.04 to 3.70% of the whole weight (Ramsey et al., 1965). According to Reichert and Brown (1909), these amounts are less than half the total blood in the body.

working position, so just gut the animal where he lies. That's where the 50 feet of cord comes in—to pull and tie legs out of the way as you work. That cord is almost like having a companion along to lend a helping hand. On one hunt I forgot to replace the cord in my hunting pack, and that was the day I killed an elk. By the time I'd finished gutting and skinning that animal, while fighting the animal's legs with my free arm, my back, my head and whatever, I felt like I'd been trampled by a herd of elk.

Now comes the skinning and bagging. When you're alone never look at an elk as a whole body but rather as manageable small pieces; as parts, not as a whole. Continue to work on the animal right where it is by skinning the upper side from one end to the other. As you free the hide spread it out neatly on the ground, keeping it clean, to serve as a ground cloth for further operations. Once you've skinned the top side you may face a decision. If a packer will be coming to retrieve your elk, you might want to divide the animal into four equal parts; it's easiest to balance on horses or mules that way. If that's the case, use your saw (or hatchet, if that's what you carry) to split the animal right down the back bone from one end to the other. Then cut just behind the last rib to split the top half into elk quarters. Slip meat sacks around those to keep them clean and to keep flies off, and lay them on logs or rocks in the shade to cool. Then roll the carcass over onto the hide and skin and quarter the other half.

If you plan to pack the animal yourself any distance, you'll have to reduce it to even smaller pieces. Skin out the top side as just described, but rather than quartering the animal, dissect it. First slice right next to the backbone to remove the backstrap (loin). Cut off the front leg then fillet all of the "bacon" meat off the rib cage, and bone out the neck. These sections have a high bone-to-meat ratio and there's little sense in packing that bone around. Next either split the pelvis with your saw and remove the upper back leg, or with some careful cutting separate the hip joint and remove the back leg by slicing it loose from the pelvis. Keep you knife right next to the bone to avoid wasting meat. Now roll the carcass over and disassemble the other half the same way. This process reduces an elk to manageable pieces. You may decide to bone out the elk completely by removing bones from the front and back legs, which will reduce weight even further. As you can see from the weight-conversion chart you can reduce a bull that field dresses 437 pounds to about 200 pounds by boning it out completely. Normally I don't bone out the legs in the field because they have a low bone-to-meat ratio, and opening them up increases the potential for contamination and excessive drying.

How long can you keep an elk in the field? Without question the sooner you get an animal into controlled locker conditions the better, but if you're far in the backcountry that's often not possible. Professional meat processors age beef for two weeks at 34 to 38 degrees, and they sometimes quick-age beef at 65 degrees. Of course, that's under ideal conditions with controlled humidity, constant temperatures and no contamination—conditions you can't match in the field—but that gives you some idea of the parameters involved in meat storage. Ray Field goes by the axiom that "life begins at 40 degrees." If you can cool meat below that temperature—that's internal meat temperature, not air temperature—then you can safely hang an animal in camp for at least a week or more. The safe time gradually decreases with rising temperatures, and if the weather is so warm that you can't cool meat below 65 degrees, you'd better get your elk to a cooling plant and frozen within three days.

A problem in the field is that temperatures fluctuate greatly from night to day. To counteract that I generally   hang an elk at night to cool the meat thoroughly, then during the day I take it down and wrap it in a tarp and cover it with sleeping bags. Sleeping bags act much as a refrigerator to keep the meat cold, and temperature of the meat generally won't rise more than a few degrees during the day if it's well wrapped. On hunts when the temperature was dropping to 40 at night and rising to 60 during the day, I've kept elk in camp for more than a week using this method and have never had a problem with meat spoilage.

Appendix A: Addresses

ADDRESSES

The addresses here will get you started in planning. These are major offices for each state and region, and from these you can get the addresses and phone numbers for all lower offices.

STATE WILDLIFE OFFICES

From state wildlife agencies you can obtain current hunting regulations, information sources such as the names of biologists, maps of state-owned hunting lands, and in most cases, a list of guides and outfitters in that state. Elk hunting is very limited in Nevada and California, but for the sake of completeness I've listed addresses for these as well as the major elk states and provinces.

Game and Fish Department
2222 W. Greenway Road
Phoenix, AZ 85023
(602) 942-3000

Division of Wildlife
6060 Broadway
Denver, CO 80216
(303) 825-1192

Department of Fish and Game
1416 Ninth Street
Sacramento, CA 95814
(916) 445-3531

Fish and Game Department
600 S. Walnut
P.O. Box 25
Boise, ID 83707
(208) 334-3700

Department of Fish, Wildlife and Parks
1420 East Sixth
Helena, MT 59601
(406) 449-2535

Department of Wildlife
P.O. Box 10678
Reno, NV 89520
(702) 784-6214

Game and Fish Department
Villagra Building
Santa Fe, NM 87503
(505) 827-2923

Department of Fish & Wildlife
P.O. Box 3503
Portland, OR 97208
(503) 229-5551

Division of Wildlife Resources
1596 W.N. Temple
Salt Lake City, UT 84116
(801) 533-9333

Department of Game
600 N. Capitol Way
Olympia, WA 98504
(206) 753-5700

Game and Fish Department
Cheyenne, Wy 82002
(307) 777-7631

Energy & Natural Resources
Fish & Wildlife Division
8th Floor, South Tower Petroleum Plaza
9915-108 Street
Edmonton, AB T5K 2C9
(403) 427-6750

Fish and Wildlife Branch
Ministry of Environment
Parliament Buildings
Victoria, B.C. V8V 1X4
(604) 387-5921

U.S. FOREST SERVICE

From these central offices you can get a complete list of National Forests for each region. There is a nominal cost for these maps.

Region 1 (Montana, Northern Idaho)
Federal Building
Missoula, MT 89807
(406) 329-3316

Region 2 (Colorado, part of Wyoming)
11177 W. 8th Avenue
P.O. Box 25127
Lakewood, CO 80225
(303) 234-3711

Region 3 (Arizona, New Mexico)
Federal Building
517 Gold Avenue S.W.
Albuquerque, NM 87102
(505) 766-2401

Region 4 (Nevada, Utah, Southern Idaho, Western Wyoming)
Federal Building
324 25th Street
Ogden, UT 84401
(801) 626-3201

Region 5 (California)
630 Sansome Street
San Francisco, CA 94111
(415) 556-4310

Region 6 (Oregon, Washington)
319 S.W. Pine Street
P.O. Box 3623
Portland, OR 97208
(503) 221-3625

BUREAU OF LAND MANAGEMENT

Ask for a free State Index Map. These list all BLM maps for each state. Prices vary but most maps cost about $2. For free Index

Maps, write to Bureau of Land Management, State Office at the following addresses:

2400 Valley Bank Center
Phoenix, AZ 85073
(602) 261-3873

Federal Building, Room E-2841
2800 Cottage Way
Sacramento, CA 95825
(916) 484-4676

Colorado State Bank Building
1600 Broadway
Denver, CO 80202
(303) 837-4325

398 Federal Building
550 West Fort Street
Boise, ID 83724
(208) 384-1401

222 N. 32nd Street
P.O. Box 30157
Billings, MT 59107
(406) 657-6462

Federal Building. Room 3008
300 Booth Street
Reno, NV 89509
(702) 784-5451

Federal Building
South Federal Place
Santa Fe, NM 87501
(505) 988-6217

(Oregon and Washington)
729 N.E. Oregon Street
P.O. Box 2965
Portland, OR 97208
(503) 231-6281

University Club Building
136 S. Temple
Salt Lake City, UT 84111
(801) 524-5311

2515 Warren Avenue
P.O. Box 1828
Cheyenne, WY 82001
(307) 778-2326

TOPOGRAPHIC MAPS

First ask for free state order maps, then from those order the specific state, regional, county or quadrangle topographic maps to cover your hunting areas.

Branch of Distribution
U.S. Geological Survey
Federal Center
Denver, CO 80225
(303) 234-3832

CONSERVATION DIRECTORY

An invaluable source of information sources is the Conservation Directory. It lists addresses, phone numbers and the names of contacts in all state and provincial wildlife agencies; offices for federal land management agencies; private conservation groups throughout North America, and much more. This book is a must for anyone seriously planning a hunt. Contact:

National Wildlife Federation
1412 Sixteenth Street, N.W.
Washington, D.C. 20036
(202) 797-6800
(As of 1983, the price was $9 plus $1.55 postage)

Appendix B: Calls and Tapes

CALLS AND TAPES

The following companies make elk calls and instructional tapes. Because prices change so rapidly, I've simply listed the type of product and will let you investigate beyond that point.

Old Jake Products
Pawlet, VT 05761
(802) 325-3017
("The Imitator" game call, an exterior diaphragm call with grunt tube.)

"Challenger" Elk Call
H.G. Jones
P.O. Box 3272
Boise, ID 83703
(208) 939-0340
(The "Challenger" Elk Call, a modified whistle with grunt tube; plus instruction tape on use of The Challenger, which includes general elk-hunting tips.)

Scotch Game Call Co., Inc.
60 Main Street
Oakfield, NY 14125
(716) 948-5242
(The Scotch #5100 Elk Call, a curley-cue type bugle.)

Burnham Bros. Wildlife Calls
Marble Falls, TX 78654
(817) 693-3112
(E-12 elk call, a traditional elk whistle made of flexible tubing; tape of two live bulls bugling. These are nasty-sounding bulls, so if you want to practice some off-beat bugling, this tape is ideal.)

Larry D. Jones
Wilderness Sound Productions
2549 N. 31st Street
Springfield, OR 97477
(503) 741-0263
(Metal-reed call with detachable reed head and grunt tube; diaphragm mouth calls; tapes with instructions on how to blow these calls as well as bugle with your voice, and general tips on bugling in a bull. Tapes also have the sounds of live bulls bugling in the field.)

Wayne Carlton's Hunting Accessories
P.O. Box 1746
Montrose, CO 81402
(303) 249-8456
(Mouth diaphragm calls; instructional tape on how to use mouth diaphragms. Tape includes two excellent sequences recorded in the field as Carlton bugles in two different bulls.)

Loren Butler
Mountain Scent and Bugle Manufacturing
P.O. Box 545
Stevensville, MT 59870
(406) 777-3920
(Traditional whistle; grunt tubes; mouth diaphragms. Two instructional tapes with tips on bugling, calling in a bull, and recorded live sounds of bulls, cows and calves in the field.)

Johnny Stewart
P.O. Box 7594
Waco, TX 76710
(817) 772-3261
(Tape of recorded live bulls in the field.)

Martin Archery
Route 5, Box 127
Walla Walla, WA 99362
(509) 529-2554
(Elk call #794--"curly--cue" bugle.)

P.S. Olt Company
P.O. Box 550
Pekin, IL 61554
(309) 348-3633
(EL-45 elk call, a traditional elk whistle, instructional record.)

MAKING A CALL

The simplest call to make is a "**curly-cue**" bugle. You simply buy a 20-inch length of ½-inch flexible gas pipe—the kind used to hook up butane gas tanks—and curl it into a tight coil. Then blow on it. As you increase air pressure you should get an ascending series of shrill notes.

You can make a traditional elk whistle out of ¾-inch garden hose or plastic PVC pipe 12 to 15 inches long. Cut one end off at an angle, and notch the top side of the pipe about an inch from that end. Make a plug that fits into the angled end of the pipe and extends back just to the notch. Flatten the top of the plug to form an air passage of about ⅛-inch between the top of the plug and the pipe. Now insert the plug into the pipe and blow. Experiment a little to get the plug just right for the best tone. Consult the diagram for details.

To blow this call, hold your hand tightly over the square end of the pipe and blow into the angled end. Blow from your stomach to get good strong pressure. By increasing air pressure you will create an ascending series of shrill notes.

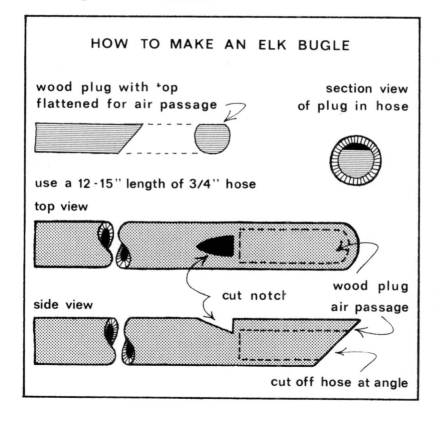

HOW TO MAKE AN ELK BUGLE

wood plug with top flattened for air passage

section view of plug in hose

use a 12-15" length of 3/4" hose

top view

side view

cut notch

wood plug

air passage

cut off hose at angle

Appendix C: A State-by-State Glance

A STATE-BY-STATE GLANCE AT ELK HUNTING

It would take an entire book to detail all hunting opportunities, so here I'll give only a brief overview of conditions in the major elk hunting states and provinces. For specifics on each state, follow the planning menu outlined in Chapter 1, and see Appendix A for addresses of pertinent management agencies and map sources.

The two "As" of elk hunting—Alberta and Arizona—stand out for trophy elk. That almost seems odd when you consider their low elk harvest and the fact that they lie at opposite ends of the elk's range. Maybe Arizona biologist Allen Guenther explained it when he said that animals often grow to greatest size at the margins, the periphery, of their range. ALBERTA has an estimated elk population of 18,000 to 20,000 animals and an annual harvest of about 1,300. Many states have a harvest 10 times that, yet Alberta, with 29 entries, ranks third behind only Montana and Wyoming in the number of elk listed in the Boone and Crockett record book ("Records of North American Big Game, 8th Edition, 1981"). In terms of percentages, then, Alberta appears to present the best potential for a huge bull. However, Alberta wildlife biologist Mike Watson said that his province has changed drastically the past 10 to 15 years, so the great hunting reflected by the record books is fast dwindling. That's particularly true in Big Game Management Unit 7 which borders Banff and Jasper National Parks. Watson said that the dense spruce and lodgepole pine country around the Ram and Panther rivers, which has produced many trophy bulls, has been opened up with roads for seismic operations and oil exploration and, as a result, the quality of hunting has declined. Watson said some of Alberta's best trophy hunting now lies along the crest of the Rocky Mountains in Units 9 and 10, directly north of the Montana border. Much of this region is roadless. Most of Alberta's general rifle seasons encompass all of September, and in some units the season is much longer. Watson said that Alberta is considering, at the time of this writing, a pre-rifle bow season throughout the province. The major fly in Alberta's hunting ointment is that all nonresidents must hunt with a Class A guide. In other words, you can't hunt on your own. You can get a list of outfitters from the Fish and Wildlife Division of Energy and Natural Resources.

ARIZONA has an estimated 20,000 elk with an annual harvest of about 2,000, which again is relatively low when you consider that some states have a harvest greater than 20,000. Despite its small elk population, Arizona produces a disproportionate number of trophy animals. Geography and vegetation may account for that in part, but also, all elk hunting in Arizona has been on a strict quota basis for many years, which assures a good carryover of mature bulls. At this writing three of the top four bulls listed by Pope and Young come from Arizona, and the Boone and Crockett record book lists 18 Arizona elk. Other states and provinces have more entries, but none except Alberta has as many in relation to the annual harvest. Topography and climate severely limit the range of elk in Arizona. The Mogollon Rim, which extends roughly from Flagstaff southeast to the New Mexico border, serves as the core of Arizona's elk habitat. Major concentrations of animals are found in units 6A and 5B just east of Flagstaff, which is high, parklike country covered with open ponderosa pine and grass, but that country is fairly heavily hunted even during the early bow season, so that's not necessarily where you'll find the best bugling. Many of Arizona's elk live year around in country that generally is considered strictly winter range, and even during September bowhunters kill large bulls in pinion-juniper lowlands surrounding the Mogollon rim and in marginal country extending north to the Grand Canyon. The Fort Apache Indian Reservation, which covers much of the Mogollon Rim region, offers perhaps the finest trophy potential found anywhere today if you can afford the price. In 1982 Dr. S. Douglas Hewette, Jr. killed a bull there that unofficially scored 394-6/8 and hunters have taken many bulls there, as well as throughout Arizona for that matter, that score in the 350 class. Early-season hunting in Arizona generally has been restricted to bow and arrow, but now some units are being opened to muzzleloaders. The bow and muzzleloader seasons run for about the last two weeks in September, and a limited number of tags are issued by drawing. Virtually all of Arizona's elk country is accessible by road, and most of it is public land.

BRITISH COLUMBIA isn't renowned for its elk hunting, but this province has excellent potential. Biologist Wally McGregor estimates the total number at about 25,000. Some 3,000 Roosevelt elk live on Vancouver Island, where only residents are allowed to hunt these animals. McGregor said that the Peace-Omineca region in the northeast corner of the province holds about 7,000 Rocky Mountain elk. Winter weather and wolves are hard on elk in this region, McGregor said, but controlled burning and transplanting of animals has helped build up herds there. The Peace River country is very remote and generally must be hunted either by boat or horseback. McGregor said the Kootenay region, a complex of mountains in the extreme southeast corner, holds about 15,000 elk. Road access is limited, McGregor said, and good soils, controlled burning and range improvement projects have enhanced this country for elk. McGregor said elk numbers have doubled here in the past 15 years, and the region now produces many trophy bulls, some in the Boone and Crockett class. The general rifle season in most of British Columbia runs from September 10 through October 20. Nonresidents face the same obstacle here as in Alberta--they must hire a guide. The Fish and Wildlife Branch, Ministry of Environment, will supply a list of guides and outfitters.

For sheer numbers, COLORADO ranks as the granddaddy of elk states. In 1982, hunters in Colorado killed more than 30,000 elk. Big game manager Bob Hernbrode said the elk population stands at about 160,000 animals, and those are about equally divided between the Northwest and the Southwest quarters of the state. The Northwest is characterized by very high densities of elk in islands of habitat, such as the Flat Tops Wilderness and the Grand Mesa, surrounded by large blocks of elkless land. In the southwest, total numbers are nearly as great, but here densities are lower because elk are more evenly distributed across a broad area. Most elk country in Colorado ranges in elevation from 7,000 feet to timberline at about 11,000 feet. Colorado is very popular with bowhunters, and the Pope and Young record book lists many bulls from this state, but the Boone and Crockett rifle book lists only 27 Colorado bulls, which is relatively few in proportion to the harvest. Most high-density elk areas are heavily hunted during general rifle seasons, so the turnover of bulls is rapid and trophy bulls are scarce. To stand the best chance of killing a huge bull in Colorado you have to hunt extremely rugged, nasty country--Colorado has its share--or you must hunt units where the number of rifle-season permits is limited. Hernbrode said the Division of Wildlife will be restricting harvest in more and more units to improve bull-cow ratios. Colorado's archery season runs for about a month beginning in early September, and you can buy a license across the counter anytime prior to the season. Also, a limited number of permits (about 4,000) is issued for a muzzleloader elk season, which falls in late September. You'll find plenty of elk hunting on National Forest, Bureau of Land Management and state-owned lands in Colorado, but many elk also live on private lands. Much private land in Colorado is leased to outfitters, and some ranchers allow hunting for a fee.

Compared to other elk states, IDAHO falls about in the middle with an annual harvest of 8,000 to 10,000 and 25 entries in the Boone and Crockett book. The total elk population is estimated at 60,000. Elk densities probably are highest in the Panhandle Region (Game Management Units 1-9), where rainfall is high and vegetation is dense. Roads reach into most of this heavily logged region. Central Idaho is as rugged and inaccessible as any territory in the Lower 48 states. The Selway-Bitterroot and River of No Return Wilderness areas encompass more then 3 million acres here. Law doesn't require nonresidents to hire an outfitter, but the physical nature of this region, where 20 miles compares to a city block back home, just about demands the use of horses. Elk numbers and trophy potential are high throughout the Clearwater and Salmon River drainages of central Idaho. Roads provide good access into most country south of the River of No Return Wilderness. The parklike country along the Montana border west of Yellowstone Park has high numbers of elk and access is fairly good. Except for major wilderness areas, where the general rifle season runs from September 15 into November, early-season hunting in Idaho is restricted to bow and arrow, and the archery season roughly takes in the month of September. Virtually all elk hunting in Idaho is on National Forest land. At this writing, Idaho issues 9,500 elk tags to nonresidents on a first-come, first-served basis.

The annual harvest in MONTANA averages about 15,000, and with 50 entries in the Boone and Crockett record book, Montana outshines all other states in terms of trophy hunting. The Department of Fish, Wildlife and Parks divides Montana into seven big game regions, and regions 1-4, which cover the western half of the state, hold most of the elk. Region 1, which is rainy, wet country much like the Idaho panhandle, encompasses the northwest corner. Wildlife specialist Glenn Erickson said that elk here feed on browse year around so productivity isn't real high and elk densities aren't as high as in some other regions. Largest herds in the northwest live in the Bob Marshall Wilderness and in the Coeur D' Alene and Cabinet Mountains, and plentiful refuge areas ensure some big bulls in this region. Region 2, which lies against the Idaho border and takes in most of west-central Montana, has high numbers of elk and generally the country is more open than in Region 1. Erickson said elk numbers are increasing in mountains surrounding the Bitterroot Valley. Region 3 includes the southwest corner of Montana and the territory surrounding Yellowstone National Park. Erickson said that open, grassy ranges here, opposed to the browse habitat of Regions 1 and 2, yield high calf production and high densities of elk. Because this is high-production country, much of it is heavily hunted and the proportion of trophy bulls remains low, but some mountain ranges, such as the Madison, Gallatin and Absaroka, have extensive backcountry and produce some huge animals. Montana's Region 3 probably has produced more Boone and Crockett bulls than any other single area. Region 4 is relatively dry open country similar to

Region 3 although the mountains aren't as high and rugged. Animal densities are high in most mountain ranges and the region produces some big bulls. The current Pope and Young world record, killed by Dave Snyder, came from the Belt Mountains in Region 4. Elk herds have grown rapidly along the breaks of the Missouri River, and bowhunters in particular have found excellent hunting in the open pine breaks of the C.M. Russell National Wildlife Refuge. Some private land holds good elk hunting, especially around major valleys, but National Forest land offers more opportunities than any hunter could explore in a lifetime, and Montana promises a good mix of backcountry and near-road hunting. The archery season runs from early-September through mid-October, and in some major wilderness areas the general rifle season runs from September 15 through November. Montana sells 17,000 nonresident elk licenses, first-come, first-served.

In NEW MEXICO the Game and Fish Department estimates elk numbers at about 15,000, and the annual harvest is about 2,000. Even though herds are growing, hunter numbers have outstripped elk herds and all general elk licenses are now limited in number to restore quality to New Mexico's elk hunting. That's good news for early-season hunters, because it means more mature bulls in the field, which ought to improve bugle hunting. Elk numbers are stable in the mountains east and north of Santa Fe, and populations are growing on the west side of the Carson National Forest near Chama and on the Gila National Forest in the southwest corner of the state. The Gila and Santa Fe National Forests offer some good wilderness hunting. New Mexico has gained a reputation for trophy elk hunting largely from the hunting on private and Indian lands. The Vermejo Park near Raton and the Jicarilla and Mescalero Apache Indian Reservations unquestionably hold some of the finest trophy elk hunting in North America for the hunter who can pay the price. New Mexico's early-season bow hunt runs for two weeks starting the second weekend in September, and the number of licenses is unlimited.

OREGON normally has ranked No. 2 behind Colorado in terms of the number of elk killed with an annual harvest of about 20,000. Despite that high kill only six Oregon elk are listed in the Boone and Crockett record book. In terms of elk populations, Oregon falls into halves divided by the Cascade Range. The West Side consists of dense rain forest and steep, low elevation mountains and the animals here are Roosevelt elk, which make up about one-third of the annual elk harvest in Oregon. The Nos. 1 and 2 Roosevelt elk listed by the Pope and Young club come from the Coast Range of Oregon. The Tioga and Alsea units have major Roosevelt elk populations, and these animals are distributed throughout the Coast Range and parts of the Cascades. Most of Oregon's Roosevelt elk country is heavily logged and road access is virtually unlimited. East of the Cascades, greatest concentrations of elk live in the Blue and Wallowa mountains and adjoining ranges. Grant County consistently produces the largest bulls, but highest elk densities are found in units bordering Washington and Idaho. Roads penetrate most of eastern Oregon's best elk range, but the Three Sisters Wilderness in the Cascade Range and the Eagle Cap Wilderness and other small roadless areas do offer good backcountry hunting. Most of Oregon's best elk hunting lies on National Forest land. At this writing Oregon has a four-week bowhunt that opens in late August, but that may be reduced by the Department of Fish and Wildlife. The number of bowhunting licenses is unlimited in most units, and these can be bought across the counter any time prior to the season.

From 1960 to 1980 elk herds nearly doubled in UTAH to an estimated 12,000 animals. The Division of Wildlife Resources plans to raise that to 20,000 by 1990. The Manti country of central Utah and the Bear Lake region in the north have the most stable elk herds. Elk are increasing in the Uintas, a very high mountain range near the Wyoming border, and new herds have been created by transplanting near Moab, Cedar City and in mountain ranges along the Nevada border. Elk are hit pretty heavy in general-season areas, so Utah isn't the best place to look for a trophy bull, and bugling opportunities are fairly limited. The two-week general archery season falls about the last week in August and the first week in September, which catches just the front edge of the rut. Some limited-quota rifle hunts held in mid-September provide good bugling opportunities, but these are restricted to Utah residents only.

The Department of Game estimates WASHINGTON'S elk population at 58,000, and the annual kill runs about 12,000. As in Oregon, the Cascade Range divides Washington into halves. East side Rocky Mountain elk are stable at about 24,000 animals. Major herds are located in the Blue Mountains and Snake River drainage in the extreme southeast corner and in the Cascade Range west and north of Yakima. On the west side Roosevelt elk continue to increase as logging opens up old-growth timber, and since 1930 the population there has jumped from 10,000 to about 34,000. Large numbers of Roosevelt elk live in the Cascade Range around Rainier National Park, in the extreme southwest corner of the state, and on the Olympic Peninsula. As of this writing the Boone and Crockett record book lists only two bulls from Washington, but that will change when the new category of Roosevelt elk, recently adopted by Boone and Crockett, shows up in the record books. A large share of the bulls will be from Washington. Eighteen of the 24 Roosevelt elk listed by the Pope and Young Club in *Bowhunting Big Game Records of North America, 1981,* come from Washington. Long Island in Willapa Bay has long been famous for its bowhunting for Roosevelt elk. Washington traditionally has offered the poorest early-season opportunities of any western state. At this writing, the Department of Game has proposed bow seasons that would open September 10 for several West Side units, but most of Washington is closed to early-season hunting.

WYOMING consistently yields the highest general-season success—from 30 to 40 percent—of any state or province, and 42 bulls, second only to Montana, are listed from this state in the Boone and Crockett record book. Annual harvest is 15,000 or more. Big game specialist Harry Harju said the famous Jackson region and the backcountry west of Cody have both high densities of elk and good trophy animals. The Bighorn Mountains near Sheridan have good numbers of elk, and even though roads penetrate much of this country, terrain here is so tough that some good trophy bulls survive. An archery-only season in parts of the Bighorns lasts all of September. Harju said the mountains of Southeast Wyoming, such as Laramie Peak, and the Snowy and Sierra Madre ranges hold thriving elk herds, but because of heavy hunting pressure the proportion of trophy bulls is lower than in more remote parts of Wyoming. The Wind River, Wyoming, and Salt River ranges in southwest Wyoming all have good numbers of elk with high trophy potential. About the only forested range in Wyoming that doesn't grow a lot of elk, Harju said, is the west side of the Tetons along the Idaho border. In wilderness areas around Jackson and Yellowstone Park, the general rifle season opens September 10 and runs through November, and throughout the rest of the state bow seasons fall during the rut. With only a few exceptions, you can hunt bugling bulls just about anywhere in Wyoming that elk exist. The big obstacle for nonresidents is that Wyoming issues only about 6,500 nonresident elk licenses by drawing, and the odds are roughly 2 to 1 against drawing a tag. Wyoming also has a ridiculous law that says nonresidents can't hunt designated wilderness areas unless they're accompanied by a guide, so if you plan to hunt on your own, don't plan to hunt designated wilderness. Harju said the only private-land obstacles exist on Laramie Peak, in parts of the Wind River Range and at the south end of the Bighorn Mountains. Otherwise most of Wyoming's best elk hunting takes place on public lands.

Appendix D: Hunting Equipment

I've listed here only items for basic hunting. Those items listed for the hunting pack go with me whenever I'm hunting. For general camping I've listed only backpacking equipment because backpacking serves as the lowest common demoninator; it involves the minimum of equipment mandatory for any hunt. For car or horse camping I'd take the same basic equipment only in greater quantity and size.

My hunting pack always includes these items:
1. Flashlight (one battery turned backwards to prevent draining of batteries; spare batteries; spare bulb.)
2. Map and compass.
3. Fire-starting materials (matches, butane lighter.)
4. 1 mil plastic tarp for emergency shelter.
5. Knife.
6. Sharpening stone or small steel.
7. Small folding saw.
8. First aid kit (bandaids, gauze, aspirin, moleskin, tube of antibiotic—eg. Polysporin.)
9. 50 feet of nylon cord.
10. Whistle (for emergency signaling.)
11. Plastic flagging (for marking trail to and from meat, etc.)
12. Elk quarter bags.
13. Lunch and high-energy foods.
14. At times my hunting pack also might include raingear, extra eyeglasses, water bottle, camera and film, wool shirt or down vest.

For bivouac hunting I would stuff the following items into a rucksack to carry in addition to the above items, which always go with me in a fanny pack:

1. 2-pound down sleeping bag.
2. Bivvy sack for shelter.
3. Soap and wash cloth.
4. Tooth brush.
5. Small aluminum pot.
6. Spoon.
7. Gasoline or sterno stove.
8. Sock hat (to keep warm while sleeping.)
9. About 1 pound of food per day.

Following is a list of items I'd take on the average backpack hunting trip. These items would be in addition to the gear already listed above, which would go with me on every hunt:

1. Elk calls.
2. Binoculars.
3. Rope for camp use.
4. Camouflage face paint.
5. Bow with 1 dozen hunting arrows and 5 practice arrows.
6. Extra pre-sharpened broadheads.
7. Finger tab and arm guard.
8. Extra bow string.
9. Bow string wax.
10. Extra arrow rest for bow.
(The rifle hunter would replace items 5-10 with rifle and ammunition.)
11. Hunting boots or shoes and light shoes for camp wear.
12. Socks—3 pairs light, 3 pairs heavy wool.
13. 2 t-shirts.
14. 2 underwear.
15. 3 hankies.
16. Wool shirt and pants.
17. Cotton camouflage shirt and pants (in predictably hot situations).
18. Wool gloves.
19. Camouflage hat.
20. Wool sock hat.
21. Down jacket for camp use.
22. Wool scarf.
23. Raingear.
24. Two-man tent.
25. Nylon or plastic tarp for lean-to shelter.
26. Foam sleeping pad.
27. Sleeping bag.
28. Gasoline stove.
29. Matches.

30. Quart pot and handle.
31. Fork, cup and plate.
32. Dish cloth and soap.
33. Alarm clock (wrist alarm chronograph.)
34. Assorted plastic bags.
35. Towel and soap.
36. Nylon twine for general camp use.
37. Notebook and pens.
38. Toothbrush and paste.
39. Toilet paper.
40. Sweat band.
41. Comb.
42. Thermometer (for checking meat temperature).
43. Flashlight for camp use.
44. Packframe and packsack.
45. Extra pins and keepers for packframe.
46. Candles for light in tent.
47. Leader and hooks for fishing.
48. Camera, lenses, film.
  49. Food (My backpacking menu generally includes granola or oatmeal cereal for breakfast; hardrolls or flour tortillas, cheese, dried beef for lunch; Mountain House freese-dried dinners for dinner; plus gorp—raisins, nuts, chocolate candies—and jerky for snacking food during the day.)

Appendix E: Trophy Scoring

IDENTIFYING A TROPHY ELK

The following prescription for judging a trophy head in the field, written by Michael C. Cupell, was borrowed from *Bowhunting in Arizona, First Edition, 1980,*   3302 El Tovar, Tucson, AZ 85705. Copies of this book can be ordered at $20 apiece.

"·A knowledge of certain basic body measurements allows a hunter to make a quick judgment of an elk's rack in the field. A mature bull is about 22''-24'' thick (side-to-side), and will be between 36''-40'' shoulder top-to-brisket. Distance from antler base to nose is usually 15''-16''. An elk with a rack that is at least half again as wide as body width, at least as high above the head as the shoulder-to-brisket distance, six tines on each antler with the first three tines as long as the distance from antler butt-to-nose, a fourth tine ⅓ again as long as this distance, and fifth tine at least 8'' long is a mature bull that would rank in about the middle of the bowhunter's record books. A very large trophy bull will have a rack that is about twice as wide as the body, easily higher above the bull's head as the shoulder-to-brisket distance, six or more tines on each antler, the first three tines longer than the antler butt-to-nose distance, a fourth tine that seems to go up forever, a fifth tine as long as the third tine, and the length of the main beam past the fifth tine longer than the length of the fifth tine. Quick rule of thumb: If the first two tines on each antler stick out to the nose, then curl up, you are looking at a biggie! Don't pass him up because he's probably the biggest bull on the mountain."

MEASURING ELK ANTLERS

This scoring chart was provided courtesy of the Boone and Crockett Club:

OFFICIAL SCORING SYSTEM FOR NORTH AMERICAN BIG GAME TROPHIES

Records of North American Big Game

BOONE AND CROCKETT CLUB

205 South Patrick Street
Alexandria, Virginia 22314

WAPITI

Kind of Wapiti _____

Minimum Score:
Roosevelt 290
American 375

DETAIL OF POINT MEASUREMENT

		Abnormal Points	
		Right	Left

	Column 1	Column 2	Column 3	Column 4
Total to E	Spread Credit	Right Antler	Left Antler	Difference

		R.	L.
SEE OTHER SIDE FOR INSTRUCTIONS			
A.	Number of Points on Each Antler		
B.	Tip to Tip Spread		
C.	Greatest Spread		
D.	Inside Spread of Main Beams	Credit may equal but not exceed length of longer antler	

IF Spread exceeds longer antler, enter difference.

—158—

E.	Total of Lengths of all Abnormal Points		
F.	Length of Main Beam		
G-1.	Length of First Point		
G-2.	Length of Second Point		
G-3.	Length of Third Point		
G-4.	Length of Fourth (Royal) Point		
G-5.	Length of Fifth Point		
G-6.	Length of Sixth Point, if present		
G-7.	Length of Seventh Point, if present		
H-1.	Circumference at Smallest Place Between First and Second Points		
H-2.	Circumference at Smallest Place Between Second and Third Points		
H-3.	Circumference at Smallest Place Between Third and Fourth Points		
H-4.	Circumference at Smallest Place Between Fourth and Fifth Points		

TOTALS

ADD	Column 1		
	Column 2		
	Column 3		
	Total		
SUBTRACT Column 4			
FINAL SCORE			

Exact locality where killed

Date killed   By whom killed

Present owner

Address

Guide's Name and Address

Remarks: (Mention any abnormalities or unique qualities)

I certify that I have measured the above trophy on _____ 19 ___

at (address) _____ City _____ State _____

and that these measurements and data are, to the best of my knowledge and belief, made in accordance with the instructions given.

Signature: _____

Witness: _____   OFFICIAL MEASURER [   ][   ][   ]

INSTRUCTIONS FOR MEASURING WAPITI

All measurements must be made with a ¼-inch flexible steel tape to the nearest one-eighth of an inch. Wherever it is necessary to change direction of measurement, mark a control point and swing tape at this point. Enter fractional figures in eighths, without reduction. Official measurements cannot be taken for at least sixty days after the animal was killed.

A. Number of Points on Each Antler. To be counted a point, a projection must be at least one inch long and its length must exceed the width of its base. All points are measured from tip of point to nearest edge of beam as illustrated. Beam tip is counted as a point but not measured as a point.

B. Tip to Tip Spread is measured between tips of main beams.

C. Greatest Spread is measured between perpendiculars at a right angle to the center line of the skull at widest part whether across main beams or points.

D. Inside Spread of Main Beams is measured at a right angle to the center line of the skull at widest point between main beams. Enter this measurement again in Spread Credit column if it is less than or equal to the length of longer antler; if longer, enter longer antler length for Spread Credit.

E. Total of Lengths of all Abnormal Points. Abnormal points are those nontypical in location (such as points originating from a point or from bottom or sides of main beam) or pattern (extra points, not generally paired). Measure in usual manner and enter in appropriate blanks.

F. Length of Main Beam is measured from lowest outside edge of burr over outer curve to the most distant point of what is, or appears to be, the main beam. The point of beginning is that point on the burr where the center line along the outer curve of the beam intersects the burr, then following generally the line of the illustration.

G-1-2-3-4-5-6-7. Length of Normal Points. Normal points project from the top or front of the main beam in the general pattern illustrated. They are measured from nearest edge of main beam over outer curve to tip. Lay the tape along the outer curve of the beam so that the top edge of the tape coincides with the top edge of the beam on both sides of the point to determine the baseline for point measurement. Record point length in appropriate blanks.

H-1-2-3-4. Circumferences are taken as detailed for each measurement.
* * * * * * * * * * * * * *

FAIR CHASE STATEMENT FOR ALL HUNTER-TAKEN TROPHIES
To make use of the following methods shall be deemed as UNFAIR CHASE and unsportsmanlike, and any trophy obtained by use of such means is disqualified from entry for Awards.
    I.   Spotting or herding game from the air, followed by landing in its vicinity for pursuit;
   II. Herding or pursuing game with motor-powered vehicles;
  III. Use of electronic communications for attracting, locating or observing game, or guiding the hunter to such game;
  IV. Hunting game confined by artificial barriers, including escape-proof fencing; or hunting game transplanted solely for the purpose of commercial shooting.
****

I certify that the trophy scored on this chart was not taken in UNFAIR CHASE as defined above by the Boone and Crockett Club. I further certify that it was taken in full compliance with local game laws of the state, province, or territory.
Date _____ _____
                                    Signature of Hunter
(Have signature notarized by a Notary Public)

THE RECORD BOOKS

Trophy record books not only make for interesting reading but they're invaluable in helping you plan a hunt:

Records of North American Big Game, 8th Edition, 1981   Boone and Crockett Club
205 South Patrick St.
Alexandria, VA 22314
(703) 548-7727
($31.50 postpaid)

Bowhunting Big Game Records of North America, 2nd Edition, 1981
Pope and Young Club
6471 Richard Avenue
Placerville, CA 95667
(916) 621-1133
($20 postpaid)

Season of the Elk
By Dean Krakel II
The Lowell Press
Box 1877
115 East 31st Street
Kansas City, MO 64141

Elk of North America
Compiled and edited by Jack Ward Thomas and Dale E. Toweill
Stackpole Books
Cameron and Kelker Streets
Harrisburg, PA 17105